THE GAZEBO

Alexander Lebenstein

As told to and edited by
Don Levin

With Foreword and Afterword

authorHOUSE®

AuthorHouse™
1663 Liberty Drive, Suite 200
Bloomington, IN 47403
www.authorhouse.com
Phone: 1-800-839-8640

First published by AuthorHouse 11/24/2008

ISBN: 978-1-4389-3172-2 (sc)

Library of Congress Control Number: 2008911047

Printed in the United States of America
Bloomington, Indiana

This book is printed on acid-free paper.

To The Children... Then and Now

To All The Innocent Who Perished ... That They May Never be Forgotten

To Tolerance ...Through Education

To family, good friends, and those who strive to do good

To Life.

Because with each passing day there are fewer and fewer voices to bear witness of history, and because the World needs more heroes who are willing to speak.

DEDICATION

I have told this story many times to hundreds of audiences. Now it is forever recorded in print, and it is done so in memory of all the sixty million people who perished during the darkest period of the history of mankind.

I dedicate this work to the memory of my parents, Natan and Lotte Lebenstein; to my sons David and Danny; my grandson Adam Lebenstein, and my granddaughter Lisa Lipman and her husband, Matthew; as well as my great-grandsons Bryce and Braden Alexander.

It is my hope that some day that each will read it and understand just what it was that I went through as a child and teenager and how it forever changed me.

I am now eighty one years young, and I have learned a lot in my life. I share my emotions as well as my experiences with all of you who read this account. I speak only the truth, and wish to provide you with the proof that it happened. I tell the children that I speak to in schools, "I remind you that you will be the last generation that has the opportunity to meet and to hear the historical account directly from the lips of a Holocaust survivor."

I am grateful to Don, who will help me teach the lessons of history by capturing my words on paper. This book is not just my story. It is more than just the saga of a Holocaust survivor. It is an account of history that took place in Europe from the 1930s through the end of the Second World War. We want all who read this book to realize they can draw lessons from the horror of this bloody time – learning principles of tolerance to be applied in today's troubled world.

This is still my nightmare. You learn to live with it much in the same manner as someone learns to live with hunger or a bodily injury, one day at a time. To be sure, some days are better than others. But despite the pain, being alive is Paradise.

Alex Lebenstein

TABLE OF CONTENTS

PREFACE

Like most German families of the 1920s and 1930s, mine had a very large garden where we would grow vegetables and fruits which my mother would then can and preserve for us to eat in the winter months. There were no supermarkets back then, and these gardening and canning activities were something that a family did in order to survive the winter. While the entire family was responsible for planting, weeding, and tending the garden, my contributions usually consisted of sitting there and eating the fruits of our labors.

Because of the amount of time spent down in the garden, it was also customary to have a gazebo in which we could find shelter from the sun and the elements. I have wonderful memories of our gazebo. It was a place dominated by love and devotion to our family. I would play with my sisters and my dogs. There was almost a special goodness that was present under the roof. Many a time my mother would bring us a thermos filled with coffee milk and fresh baked goods which we would all share lovingly. I remember my father playing cards with his friends – sometimes screaming at one another in excitement, their feet shifting the sand beneath the table and in front of the benches in either their excitement or frustration. Some of these friends were like blood brothers to my father, with their relationships forged and tempered on the battlefields of France during the First World War. It was a wonderful place to pass an afternoon as the air would be filled with the smell of cigars, freshly ground and brewed coffee, or of course steins full of beer.

The sun would be a source of warmth, and a gentle breeze would blow through the open sides of the gazebo keeping us comfortable, and I would often curl up on a bench and take a nap.

I remember planting seeds in the rich soil in the early spring, and watching them soon poke their heads up from the ground. In the eyes of a child, it seemed almost overnight that these sprouts would soon flower and the vines would soon begin to creep up the trellis that surrounded the gazebo, and a rich lush green forest wall would soon form. It was creation and re-creation, all to be nurtured under the hands of my family and then harvested to give us continued life. During the growing seasons, the sides and trellis of the gazebo would be covered with the beans that grew up towards the sun before we would pick them. I associate this cycle of growth with the spirit of Love, Family, and Friendship that I remember most about my early childhood. I never would have suspected before the events of *Kristallnacht* that these wonderful idyllic memories would be forever shattered and replaced by others of sheer terror that left me feeling hostile, bitter, and in extreme pain. Unfortunately it is these latter memories that continue to haunt me some seventy years later.

By November, there were no beans left, just the empty dry vines and leaves that eerily swirled and danced in the wind. They scraped themselves against the wooden beams every time the wind would blow; creating an empty sound that still sends chills up and down my spine to this very day. Of all the sights and sounds that left a lasting impression on me during the years that I fought to survive, there is no doubt that the sounds I experienced while we huddled on the gazebo after our escape from the destructive mobs that destroyed our home and took our possessions during *Kristallnacht* are the ones that will forever haunt me.

FOREWORD

As parents we all feel a desire, or even a duty, to shield our children from the vulgarity and ugliness that the world has to offer. Today, one of our largest challenges is to protect our children from the evils of images that come into our home via television and the Internet. We attempt to shield our children from these images that have the ability to first desensitize and then to forever stain their souls. Gratefully, none of us have to physically shield our children from the ravages of an existence where continued life, or the finality of death, can be decided and assigned by the mere pointing of a finger or the nod of a head.

I spent my teenaged years chasing girls, driving cars, and typically worrying about what the impact of a minor case of acne might have on my life. A voracious reader and devoted aficionado of History, I spent a great deal of time learning vicariously, through words that described the tiny sparks of good and the horror of the bad, associated with what historians now describe as the Holocaust, the Final Solution, or more vaguely, World War Two. I heard tales and saw faded photos of distant relatives from the *Old Country* who had perished in the camps, bringing some modicum of reality to the madness.

Alex Lebenstein, spent the same formative period of his life living, breathing, seeing, hearing, and feeling, the horror that was Kristallnacht, the *Ghetto*, and finally, *the Camps*, and to this day, bears the physical, mental, and emotional scars of what must assuredly be described as the most heinous chapter in the history of Man.

Amazingly, to this day, there are still those who persist in attempting to convince the world that none of this ever happened; that it was a giant hoax perpetuated by politicians. This book will dissuade anyone who ever had even a glimmer of doubt.

I remember as a child, encountering these survivors on the streets of downtown Skokie, Illinois. Skokie is located outside of Chicago and represented one of the largest concentrations of Holocaust survivors in the 1960s. I remember walking with my grandparents and viewing the odd tattoos that defaced the forearms of these people. I was told never to point or to stare, but rather allow these people to attempt to resume some form of normalcy in their lives. Alex need only flash to the recesses of his own memories to recall the satanic blood and horror that was his own childhood; the ruthless dedication of those who operated the trains, gas chambers, firing squads, and crematoria with the efficiency of a large scale corporation that ultimately led to the death of millions of people in the span of eight years as the world went temporarily mad.

I have had the opportunity to walk some of the hallowed ground in Germany where the blood of countless millions of innocents was spilled, land where neither vegetation nor insect, nor wild animals for that matter, can survive due to the still contaminated ground, poisoned by the insecticides used to kill countless people deemed "inferior" by those who viewed themselves as the master race. It is eerie to stand there and to listen to the whispers that still call from the faded and crumbling buildings; more than whispers at times, as the wind howls, filling the air with cries of mothers and children, as well as voices of those powerless to protect them or stop the killing. One can only <u>imagine</u> what it was like to be separated from his family, to suffer the agony of not knowing the fate of these loved ones. If one was fortunate enough to *know* the fate of loved ones, then one could only inwardly mourn their passing and attempt to accompany their spirit out of this mortal life by keeping them in our thoughts, and thereafter remain focused on the sole goal of our own survival. Alex knew the fate of his father, but had to cling to the hope that his mother would survive so that they could be reunited at war's end.

Now it is my honor to assist Alex, who actually lived it, and who will never ever forget the faces, the sounds, or the smells, as they remain forever emblazoned in his memories; who now desires to tell his story before his own life ends, so that the children will know. It is a story important enough for all of us to learn and to remember, and to share with the children of future generations. There have been many books written on this subject, and like other aspects of our history, this one too is gathering dust. The very essence of the Truth, as well as the eyewitness stories fraught with the emotion and passion of these times, is being lost to future generations with each passing day as more and more of those who lived this horror leave this life.

The tragedy is that the natural man is an enemy of God, and if he does not know of his history, he will be destined to repeat it. For this reason, this unique story must be recorded, and added alongside the accounts of others, that the children will know, and that the memories of millions who perished will be honored, and future generations will be spared the blood and horror of a time when the world truly went mad.

Both Alex and I are fathers and grandfathers. Alex is even a very proud and grateful great-grandfather. I am approaching the middle years of my journey through life, while Alex the twilight years. A chance meeting brought us together, and afforded us the opportunity to collaborate on this book as a memorial to those who were murdered and as a warning to future generations.

This is one man's story of survival and subsequent re-birth. It is intended as both a testimony and a legacy; an accounting of the triumph of good over evil, and how the will to survive can burn brightly even in a world filled with darkness. It is also a story of how faith can be restored, and the manner by which the power and influence of children present and future can bring about change for the better in our world. It is a story of the beauty and innocence of children and the influence that they can be and why it is still possible to have hope for the future.

More than anything else, this is the amazing life story of the sole survivor of the entire Jewish community of the town of Haltern am See, Germany. It is the legacy that he now shares with thousands of children in both the United States and in the Federal Republic of Germany, and through them, with generations to come.

Don Levin

INTRODUCTION

Today, a visitor to the North Rhine – Westphalia region of Germany can marvel at the beauty and serenity that radiates from the region. While heavily industrialized in parts, there is still a great deal of rural forested area, as well as a two thousand year history that one can trace on foot, on bicycle, or at high speeds on the highest density of roadways found anywhere in Germany.

Bounded on the west by Belgium and Holland, this is the most densely populated region of Germany, with nearly one in five Germans living within this area[1]. While the towns of Dortmund, Essen, Aachen, and Muenster bear names that may be recognized by many foreigners, there is a town nestled among these better known cities known as Haltern am See, or roughly translated, Holding at the Lake.

Two thousand years ago Romans marched here, and on a 315 kilometer route between Xanten and Detmold were denied access to the Northern regions of Germany. Today, one may bicycle on this path and find Roman traces in the city of Xanten and in the Roman museum in Holding at the Lake or in Begkamen Oberaden. In the museum are important archaeological findings of the last one hundred years that date back to the Emperor Augustus.

Holding at the Lake, or simply Haltern as it will be referred, with great historical roots, has something to offer everyone. From its lakeside landscape and the rivers and channels, to heath and moorland landscapes, as well as deep forests, it is beautiful in its nature, quaint in the old European sense, and teeming with the industry of the new century.

With its important past as a Roman base, the history of Haltern as a municipality can be traced back to 1289, and even further back to 1169 in church records, due to its strategic border situation at the transition between the prince diocese of Muenster and the cure principality of Cologne. Walls encircled the town with seven high military towers and town-gates. Today, only the Devil Tower (1502) remains. In the mid sixteenth century it was part of the Westfalian Hans Federation and flourished during this period. Through secularization and the Napoleonic wars, the city fell under the domain of Prussia. Never more than a medium sized town, its location in reference to water, mountains, and forest made it a pivotal location throughout history.

The Jewish cemetery on the outskirts of the town dates back to 1767. In this cemetery a tragic part of this story, Kristallnacht, will be told in chapter five. Some sixty years later, the pain and sadness of that day was partially alleviated by the children of Haltern, the children of a generation twice removed from the horrors of the events. On 26 January 1997, a memorial stone in the form of an old-testamentary law board, cut by a Halterner stone sculptor, paid for by the fundraising efforts of these same children, was placed there to atone for sins of grandparents still in denial, as well as to lay a foundation for tolerance and caring in future generations. On the granite stone are engraved the names of "Jewish citizens who were uprooted, driven away and murdered during the years 1933 to 1945." Also immortalized on that stone is the sole survivor of the Jewish community that existed on Kristallnacht, Alexander Lebenstein.

It was in the nearby city of Lembeck that Mendel Lebenstein was born in 1769 and lived a long life until 1863. Nathan Lebenstein was also born in Lembeck in 1804, and there is no record as to when this great-grandfather of Alex was put to rest.

Alexander Natan Lebenstein, Master Butcher, was also born in Lembeck on October 27, 1835. It was this man, the grandfather of Alex, who later settled the Lebenstein clan in the city of Haltern. He established his butcher shop at 36 Disselhof Strasse and was a pillar of the community until his death on December 12, 1910. It was in this city of 12,000 residents that the Lebensteins settled, and modestly prospered. In time, Alexander taught his son, Natan (Nathan) Lebenstein, who was born in Haltern on April 21, 1880, the ways of a Master Butcher.

Natan married Charlotte Josephs of the nearby town of Jever, who was known to her family and friends as Lotte. Four years younger than her husband, she was a devoted wife and mother, and wonderful partner. Natan worked diligently at his craft as a Master Butcher. They were soon blessed with three daughters, Hildegard (1915), Rosa (1918), and Alice (1920). While raising this family, the call to arms was heard in the town of Haltern, and Natan, at age 36, answered this call, and served his beloved country.

On 11 November 1918, the Great War, the War to end all Wars, ended with the signing of an Armistice between Germany and the Allies. With the abdication of Kaiser Wilhelm II at the same time, the seeds of discontent were sown in Germany. Defeated, in debt, and essentially leaderless, Germany was also being viewed as the land of opportunity for some. While nothing new, the anti-Semitic policies of the Eastern European countries, and especially Poland, had driven over 55,000 Polish Jews to the new land of opportunity in the Weimar Republic of Germany.

In December 1918, the nationalistic, anti-Semitic organization Stahlhelm (literally translated as the Steel Helmet) was established by disgruntled war veterans in Germany. As an organization, it was dedicated to restoring Germany to the position of prominence and domination that it had enjoyed under Kaiser Wilhelm II.

In 1919, the Weimar Republic was formed after the adoption of a democratic constitution. Simultaneously, the German Worker's Party (DAP) was founded in Munich. Nine months after its inception, Adolf Hitler became the party's fifty-fourth member and joined the party's executive committee as its seventh member. Within a year, the party's name had evolved to the National Socialist German Workers' Party (NSDAP) and was being led by Adolf Hitler. A contraction of the first two words newly added to the party name led party members to be known and referred to as Nazis.

In 1923, the anti-Semitic newspaper Der Sturmer (the Attacker), which came out with very pro-Nazi rhetoric, was launched. Its inaugural issue attempted to blame the then rampant inflation on the Jews, going so far as to adopt as its slogan Die Juden sind unser Ungluck which translates as the Jews are our misfortune.

Against this backdrop, and with a sense of misplaced over confidence, the Nazis attempted to take over the government, and were decidedly unsuccessful. The Munich beer hall Putsch (uprising) resulted in a prison sentence for its leaders, including Hitler. While in prison, Hitler wrote Mein Kampf (My Struggle). Using the book as a platform, Hitler outlined for the world the horror that he would unleash over the course of the next twenty years. According to Hitler, at the heart of all of Germany's ills were the Jews. They became the scapegoat for every obstacle or barrier to the resurgence of Germany.

Without citing the works of Charles Darwin, Hitler alleged that good races and bad races struggle for survival. The best race was of course the Aryan race which had people of Nordic blonde hair and blue eyed German features. The least desirable race was of course that of the Jew. Not only did Hitler advocate that to be Jewish was a religion, but that it was also a race, and a race that needed to be eradicated from the face of the Earth.

Any reader of this blueprint of horror would have known that Hitler's vision for the master race included the annihilation of what he deemed lesser, inferior races, most notably the Jews, and that the wrongs inflicted on the German people by the Treaty of Versailles would be rectified and a better life achieved for all Germans if the people would support his ideology.

This ideology was based on a single party dictatorship [to be led by Hitler himself], a state controlled economy, complete racial purity, a vigorous distinction between socialism and communism, and a strong armed forces. Once the armed forces had been restored to their proper levels, the expansion of the German state through annexations of other countries that should rightfully either be in the German sphere, or were simply required could be accomplished. This was deemed necessary in order to meet the need for Lebensraum (sufficient living space), which would in turn allow for further growth and development of the master race.

At the same time, during much of the 1920s and 1930s, the churches of Germany were continuing to spew their anti-Semitic messages, and Jewish homes were defaced and businesses were boycotted and occasionally burned.

Adding to the discontent of the general population, and most assuredly to the feelings of humiliation being felt by veterans of the War, France and Belgium occupied the Ruhr region after Germany was unable to meet its *annual payment of war reparations designed to pay off the $31 billion dollar war debt as assessed by the victorious Allies.*

With each passing setback or humiliation, the ever growing inflation and the almost worthless money, the contrived scapegoat for the Nazi Party was the Jew. Although the Jewish population within Germany was very small, it was nonetheless always identified as the source of all evil.

As the Nazis consolidated their power, attacks on Jews became even more prevalent, especially in the larger cities of Berlin, Nuremberg, and Munich. In September 1931, Jews were attacked in Berlin after having participated in services at their synagogue.

Hitler's solution to the Jewish Problem crystallized when the Protocols of the Elders of Zion, was brought to Germany by emigrants from Russia where it had first been published in 1905, to justify the persecution of Jews in that country. This vile document, later established as pure fabrication, described an alleged Jewish conspiracy to take over the world. It was read throughout Europe and even within the United States, and was actually heralded by men of influence such as Henry Ford, a noted anti-Semite.

Using this document to support his ideologies, Hitler claimed it as his license to deal with the Jewish problem once and for all, and to eradicate the Jewish people from the face of Europe. With Hitler's subsequent rise to the position of Chancellor in 1933, the die was cast.

PART I

A Real Mama's Boy

CHAPTER 1

Roots

"Politicians were a dime a dozen."

I wish I knew Americans that were as patriotic to the United States of America as my father had been to Germany. While he was a Jew by religion, he was a German through and through by nationality. He was proud to be a German, and felt a great sense of duty when he left my mother and sister and went off to France to fight on behalf of the Fatherland in World War I. Back in those days, all it took was a letter to either the city or the school informing those in charge that all 17 and 18 year old men, and/or men of an older age, were to be drafted into the Army. Quite often it was enough to cause a company or even an entire battalion to be assembled from various elements of a single town. The thought of those leading the Army at that time was that if men were drafted together from the same city or town or school, they would be that much more inclined to protect one another on the battlefield. I don't know if this was completely true, but from what I understand, my father came home from the war, a decorated, wounded veteran, with great bonds to the men with whom he had served. He was proud of the service that he had rendered, and he did come home with a very tight circle of friends. He spent the years between the World Wars working and serving them professionally on a daily basis, as well as enjoying social gatherings where they would talk and play cards. From casual friendships was born a brotherhood forged in war.

Politicians were a dime a dozen. They came and they went. None of them were very well organized or had either a politically extensive or financially secure platform from which to operate. Quite frankly, living in the city of Haltern, my parents were very insulated from the comings and goings of the politicians of the big cities. Berlin was a long way away by horse and buggy or by bicycle, and even a train ride. It really did not impact them in their own little world. I guess that is one reason that most people, my parents included, did not pay a whole lot of attention to Adolf Hitler and the Nazis. They were just another political group that would surely have their fifteen minutes in the spotlight and then fade away into the woodwork. But as time passed, and things got progressively rougher for Jews everywhere, it became apparent that Hitler and the Nazis were not going to go the way of the other political parties of that time. Yet, my father and mother still stubbornly clung to the belief that all would be well, and as an infant and then child, I knew nothing of what was transpiring in the world around me.

Chapter 2

With the Boy, There is Joy

"I didn't know from nothing."

Alexander Lebenstein was born on November 3, 1927. At the time of his birth, the small house and butcher shop at 36 Disselhof Strasse in the town of Haltern already resonated with the sounds of the three girls, Hildegard (died of natural causes in 1932), Rosa, and Alice. While it is very common today for couples to launch careers, delay marriage, and to have children after the age of forty, in the 1920s this was not only unusual, but in most cases, also quite inadvertent. Nonetheless, so it was when Natan and Lotte Lebenstein welcomed their first and only son into the world. Natan was forty-seven years of age, and Lotte forty-three. As was the custom of the Jewish people, the new parents named their son for a deceased relative, in this case, his paternal grandfather Alexander, the man who had settled the family in the city of Haltern.

A generally happy child himself, the arrival of Alex brought great joy to his parents, who would often proclaim to their friends, "With the boy, there is joy."

Haltern am See and its 12,000 inhabitants lived the very traditional small town life of 1920s and 1930s Europe. With an additional 22,000 residents coming from nearby towns, Sunday was spent in the marketplace, where oompah bands would play traditional music, and friends and families would join together to sample that week's Eintopfgericht, or loosely translated, "everything in one pot". Not musically talented, Alex enjoyed listening to the primitive radio that the family owned, as well as the live bands and theater performers that would visit the town. As the only boy in the family, not to mention being the baby as well, Alex was greatly indulged by his parents much to the chagrin of his older sisters.

It bears noting that when one dines with Alex today, his appreciation for food in any manner, shape, or form is extremely evident. More than just compensation for all the years that he was physically deprived, it is a reflection of the joy and zeal with which he continues to live his life, now in his eighty second year. This joy is contagious, and anyone who is favored to dine with Alex soon finds him to be a genial and generous host with an extremely diverse palate.

Like most children of that time, Alex did not have an inkling of the truth surrounding procreation. Between modesty and the manner in which he was sheltered by both of his parents, his was a very limited knowledge.

I was a real Mama's boy. Nothing gave me greater pleasure or security than to be with my mother. I learned all that is good from her and by her example. My mother taught me manners, as well as the rules by which to live my life.

My mother would cook pots of delicious pudding, and then hide a whole toasted almond in one of the cups that she would dish up. If you were lucky enough to be the one who received the almond in your portion of pudding, you would then be excused from that day's chores, which in those days could mean a lot of work. Aside from animals to be tended, there was always much cleaning to be done. This was in the days when dirty laundry was done by hand on a wash board, and the clothes wrung out with a hand cranked wringer, and weather permitting, hung on a clothesline to dry. This was long before washers, dryers, dishwashers, and other mechanical devices that were designed to make life easier. Life in a rural town meant lots of work for everyone. It was a natural way of life. I never thought about the chores that I was tasked to do; I merely did them. That was what all families of this time did in order to survive. There were no supermarkets back then. If a family wanted to eat in the winter, that meant working a huge vegetable garden in the warm weather, and preserving the food to be put away for the winter. In addition to the vegetable garden that my family maintained, there was also a potato field that my father leased until times got rough for him. We used to roast the odd potatoes that did not make it into the baskets, along with all the old vines and growths in a bonfire, right there in the field. The potatoes were delicious, and a real treat. Charred on the outside, the flavor of the potato was sealed inside, and greatly enhanced. Adding to the pleasure of the moment, my mother would bring us coffee milk to drink. We would sit on the ground around the fire, and it was truly a wonderful, carefree experience.

More often than not, I was the one who received the almond in my pudding. My sisters would get so mad and believed, rightfully so, that my mother was playing favorites. Sometimes I would actually give one of them, usually my sister Rosa, the almond because I felt bad for them. It also helped to keep the peace. One time my sister Alice caught me giving the almond to Rosa and wanted to beat me up. She chased me all through the house and yard and was later chastised by my mother for picking on me. It was as if I could do no wrong. I just know that I loved my mother and my father a great deal, and have many wonderful memories such as this one.

Being that I was the baby, and a boy at that, my parents did everything they could to make a happy childhood for me, and they could not get enough of me. They kept me so very happy.

I guess for that reason, I never gave my parents any reason to smack me, and generally tried to be a good kid. Of course whenever my father did try to give me a little discipline, my mother would bear down on him, and that is why she was my entire world. Aside from the puddings and other desserts that my mother would cook for us, I did not really have any favorite foods, because like most kids of that time, I ate what was put in front of me or went to bed hungry. We really were not allowed or encouraged to have favorite foods. You simply ate anything and everything that was put in front of you. This arrangement basically served to make me appreciate all foods. Of course, if I knew then what I know now, I would never have taken any form of food for granted.

The one time that my mother did take me to task was when I was around nine or ten. My mother routinely sent me to the little store in our neighborhood for the few items that she might need that day, such as dried beans or peas. These came in large sacks and were often displayed in barrels as well. The floor of the store would be full of barrels and sacks of these basic commodities, as well as ones containing roasted peanuts. Oh, how I loved roasted peanuts. They were really something that I could freak out over. I would go down with the list either in my head or on a tiny piece of paper, have it filled by the lady who ran the store, and then bring it home to my mother. I never had to worry about an exchange of money because once a week or so, my mother would go to the store and settle up her account with the owner.

Well, on this one trip to the store, I was feeling a bit mischievous, if not a little hungry, and decided that the peanuts they had in the store looked very inviting. So, I took it upon myself to make the decision that the few cents that I spent would be but a small investment in the happiness of my stomach. I took the peanuts home and was actually hoarding them in my room so as not to eat them all at once. Wouldn't you know it, but the very next day my mother went to the store for something else, and decided that so long as she was there, she would also square up with the owner. When she saw the charge for the peanuts, she said, "What is this? I never bought any peanuts."

"Oh, but Alex was here. You sent him for this item, and he bought the peanuts as well." When she was informed that I had made the purchase along with the other things that she had sent me to the store to buy, my fate was sealed. My mother paid for the peanuts and came home looking for me.

"Alex. Alexander, come over here. Did you buy peanuts? Did you buy peanuts when I sent you to the store yesterday?"

"I don't think so," I said weakly.

"Did you buy peanuts," she asked me again, a little more forcefully. "Mrs. So and So said you bought peanuts. I know that I did not tell you to buy peanuts. Did you buy peanuts?"

"Yes Mommy," I said, trying to appear cute.

"Did you eat them all?"

"No Mommy."

"Where are the peanuts? Go get them!"

So I dug out the peanuts from wherever I had them in hiding and brought them to my mother, because I knew if I did not do it, that there was going to be hell to pay.

What she did seemed extremely cruel at the time, because after confronting me with the offense, and administering the beating that she applied to my *tush*, she then proceeded to take the peanuts away from me, keeping them high up on a shelf in the kitchen where she stored the coffee as well.

My punishment was that every day she would give me just one peanut as an appetizer to my breakfast before I went to school. I refused to eat it every morning. It was such a punishment. I would cry, "I don't want it, I don't want it. I don't want to eat that one peanut. Why can't I have three or four more peanuts?"

"Because you are a bad boy, and you cannot have any more peanuts. One peanut. That is your punishment. Now eat that peanut," she would argue right back. "It will teach you a lesson!"

"I don't want to eat it, I don't want to eat it," I would wail. Or I would cry, "Why did you give me such a small peanut? At least give me a big peanut."

In any event, that was my punishment, and it took me a very, very long time to eat that bag of peanuts, exactly one peanut at a time. No matter how much I would beg and plead for more peanuts, the answer was always the same.

A punishment like that is never to be forgotten, for it taught me so much. It taught me never to lie, never to do anything that is not right to do, never to betray a trust or confidence that is given to you, and so on. It was such a deep lesson that I remember it to this day.

While I secretly enjoyed that peanut each day, it was pure torture not to put my hand into the bag and to grab a whole fistful. To this day, I still enjoy nuts of all kinds and think of my dear mother each time that I partake.

When it came to matters of procreation, I really didn't know from nothing. I didn't know anything about sex, but I knew that there was something mysterious about it. I had no idea where babies came from. I was led to believe that when a man and a woman loved one another and they were ready for a baby to join their family that they were supposed to put sugar on the window sill, and somehow, a baby would appear via the stork. Of course the stork was not always nice to the mother, and would often bite her legs which would result in varicose veins. With no movies, books, or internet to dissuade me from thinking that this was the absolute truth, it all made perfect sense. It might also explain why my sisters were always laughing and having fun at my expense. Of course I was not the only gullible one.

There is a church on a hill called Annaberg, in Haltern, where there used to be water fed by a spring running out of part of the mountain, and in turn flowing into a round stone horse trough where horses would naturally stop and drink their fill of cool clean mountain water. The story is told that during my mother's pregnancy with me, my 7-year old, gullible sister, Alice would go up there and put sugar on the lip of the horse trough for the stork to take and to then bring her a baby brother. Naturally the horses would lick the sugar away, but my sister believed that the stork had taken it.

We had a neighbor named Daniels, who had a child about one year younger than me. The mother did not have sufficient milk to nurse the child, and as was the custom of the time, my mother acted as a wet nurse, and actually nursed her baby for her. This was a challenge for my mother because I kept right on for quite a while too. To finally discourage me from the practice of nursing, my mother started putting hot mustard around her nipple. After tasting the mustard, my answer to that was to say, "More, more." It might explain why I like hot food to this day.

Play time was always outside for me. With the butcher shop and animals an integral part of our household, indoors was not the place for children to play.

I would help my mother in the kitchen while she cooked. My usual job involved "tasting" whatever she was cooking at the time. But, I really did learn quite a bit about cooking from her simply by watching.

Everyone always wants to know what my childhood was like, especially in terms of the holidays. Chanukah was vastly different than it is for modern Jewish children. It was not a major holiday full of presents like it is for children today. I might get a trinket or two, but back then, that was the way. We had no Chanukah menorahs, for we actually used plain boards with candles. Our holiday toys were not Nintendos or Gameboys, but rather *dreidels* with peanuts. We would sing the songs and say the prayers, but like today, it was not a major holiday that required us to go to the synagogue. Reformed Judaism in the United States was really brought over by the German Jews who had emigrated in the 1800's. Whereas Orthodox Jews put their faith ahead of their nationality, Reformed Jews put their nationality first. This was definitely the case with my father, who remained a very proud German Jew until it was too late.

On other holidays, as well as the Sabbath, I would accompany my family to the synagogue, and I would sit with my father on the first floor in the main chamber with all of the other men and boys, while my mother and sisters sat upstairs in the balcony. Sadly, as the Jewish population of the town dwindled due to relocation and emigration, sometimes we could not get Sabbath services organized. Because even though there were twenty families still in town, not all actively participated in worship. As a result, we often had difficulty in meeting the requirement of having ten men present to form a *minyan* (quorum required for prayer). Quite often we would invite scholars from some of the larger cities to come to instruct us and to help form the *minyan*. When this happened, they would often stay with us because we had extra rooms in our home. The fact that we had teenaged girls in the house caused the young men to prefer our home even more. I vividly remember how they would all be making "googly eyes" at one another, and I hated it. Yeuch. I often expressed my displeasure in some of the pictures that were taken by making faces or simply by kicking the shins of potential suitors for my sisters.

CHAPTER 3

Peeking From the Landing

"If not for the war and all of its horror, I may have become a bone doctor."

Up until 1934-1935, as was the custom of the day, we often had several other people living in our home at any given time. These were young people who were apprenticed to my father and were in the process of learning the [kosher] butcher trade. It was not uncommon in the course of a seven-year apprenticeship to live in with the master's family, or on the premises, for up to four years. An apprentice would work for free or very little, in exchange for room and board, while still attending school in some cases. The first four years were known as the *lehrling* (learning time), which was then followed by three years known as the *geselle* (practice). Because the butcher shop was such an integral part of our home, in order to keep the blood and other byproducts that would be on the floor of the shop from being tracked throughout the house, my mother would often put down sawdust between the shop and the kitchen table so that the men did not have to remove their work shoes, and the sawdust would absorb all the foreign matter that they brought into the house on their boots.

My father was a Master Butcher and ran quite a shop. I know this because I would often spend a great deal of time observing him as he worked. Sometimes he would even wrap a white apron around me and allow me to help out with some of the more menial chores. "Now you are in training," he would say. This sometimes included leading the sheep and smaller animals into the shop.

While the law did not allow me to be present when he was slaughtering the animals, I would often peek through the window that looked into the slaughterhouse portion of the shop from the landing of the staircase that led up to our bedrooms on the second floor. I had figured out ways to keep the wooden stairs that led down to the window from squeaking, so that I could stand there and watch the process undetected. Being that these were the days before electrical tools and machinery, the slaughtered animals were always hoisted up by hand. While the animal was still on the ground, the skin would be loosened. Once the cattle were hanging, the skin could then literally be pulled off because there were blisters that separated the skin on the back from the main carcass. This skin had to be removed before the stomach could be opened as another precaution against contaminating the meat.

Once the animal had been killed and was hanging, I was allowed to be in the shop. Many times my father called me in and made a little tool out of a giant wooden clothes pin for me to use. He then put me up on a step ladder and allowed me to help remove the skin by moving the clothes pin between the blisters. He showed me the motions and allowed me to do it. That was the kind of training that I received at the hand of my father. I was absolutely fascinated with the entire process. Not so much that the animal would be killed, but rather how God had created such an incredible beast. The way bone, muscle, tendon, and sinew were all packed together to produce a living, breathing creature absolutely fascinated me. I was particularly enthralled with the bones and joints that formed the skeleton. When my father was done with his work, I was then allowed to use my wooden knife to separate the joints. Watching the liquid cartilage run out was absolutely fascinating to me. I would then open up bones and look at the marrow and liquid that would run out of them. I started asking my father all sorts of questions, one after the other, about cartilage, and whether we had the same thing in our bones. I suspect that had my education not been disrupted by the all the events that surrounded the war, I might have some day become a bone doctor. I studied the ribs, the spinal cord, and continued to ask questions. I know that under normal circumstances I would have been a great doctor. I know that my parents would have supported my choice because I would have given it my best efforts, just as I have always done my entire life with everything I have ever undertaken.

Behind our house, we had livestock as well as chickens and my two dogs. It was not uncommon for us to also have geese in the yard and for them to weigh in excess of twenty pounds. Unfortunately, if they were that big, it was pure fat that made them so big, having been force-fed by the farmers who sold them to my father. The technique, a practice still in use today in many European countries, required nailing their webbed feet to the floor and often forcing food down their gullets after they have voluntarily stopped eating. There would be hardly any meat on the animal, but in this case, the fat was prized just as much. The liver inside the goose would be bigger than my hand. We would have liver from both geese and calves and my father would grind it into a nice chopped liver pate. He was actually quite famous for his particular recipe, and people would buy it especially on the holidays.

My father would render the goose fat by cooking and seasoning it in what, through my child's eyes, were giant woks, creating *gribnous*, or cracklings. This fat was then later used in the liver pate. I realize today that the woks were not as big as they may have appeared to a young child, but it was all so fascinating to watch the Master at work. No doubt about it, my father really was good at what he did. The smells that permeated the shop and the house are some of my favorite memories to this day.

Sometimes I think that my main purpose in life was to be my father's guinea pig. Many a morning I would start my day by having him shove something into my mouth with the order to "Taste this." For the most part, it was a wonderful experience because my father would grind the spices by hand in separate mills reserved for this purpose, and would add them in the preparation of his liverwurst, knockwurst, and salami. In the shop he had this closet in which he would keep the eight separate coffee mills in each of which he would only grind that one particular spice. I do remember that he had a "special formula" for his liverwurst, which he would grind and mix behind the door in this closet. Nobody else was allowed to know the recipe, and nobody ever did find out what it was. It was always the same wonderful taste, year in and year out. I always appreciated being the one to sample it, though it might have been nice if it was not early morning when he asked me to try it! Looking back on it today, I realize that it was also a tremendous honor that my father was affording me, and it makes me more grateful for it.

Needless to say, because our home and the butcher shop were connected, I grew up with the smells of the old-fashioned smokehouse and sausage spices, all beautiful, beautiful things. Unless something dramatic had happened that had allowed me to go to medical school, I suspect that I would otherwise have been expected to grow up to be a butcher like my father, and his father before him. That was the way of the time for the oldest, or in my case, only son.

As I said, it was absolutely fascinating to watch my father work. To be a kosher butcher was tantamount to being ordained like a rabbi; maybe not that learned, but both were skilled and knowledgeable. As a *Schochet* he was authorized to slaughter the animals in accordance with the traditions and kosher laws. For each animal to be slaughtered there was a different kind of knife. The size and sharpness of each knife had to be exactly right. I remember that each of his special knives, the *chalef*, or *chalufim* in the plural, had handles made from a ram's horn. Aside from being extremely sharp, they were also very beautiful to look at. The steel blades were rectangular, without a point. With three quick motions of the knife the animal would be dead.

Something that I really enjoyed doing was traveling to the farms with my father in our two-wheeler horse-pulled wagon. When we were ready to leave our home, my father would wrap me up in a soft woolen blanket, and when it was really cold, a leather blanket over that. While he still had a license to operate a slaughterhouse, the purpose of our trip was so that he could go out to the farm to pick the cattle that he wanted. My father would examine them, buy them, and then the farmer would deliver them to his shop in whatever time frame my father designated. After the Nazis had enacted the Nuremberg Laws that prompted the loss of my father's license, he was reduced to being a farm butcher and would have to slaughter the animals there for the farmer. To accomplish this, we would often spend the night. With the loss of his license and primary profession, this became the means by which my father supported our family. These righteous farmers would engage my father out of respect for his professional skills as well as for him as a man. Even at that young age, it was easy for me to recognize that my father was highly respected, which in turn made me even more proud of him.

I also remember that while visiting the farms, many of the farmers' wives really took a shine to me. They would give me ice cold cherries that had been chilled in the well. I can still taste them to this day. Even better than the cherries: was when a farmer's wife would churn fresh butter for the bread that had just been baked, with charcoal embers still in the bottom of the loaf.

I have to say that perhaps the most amazing thing that I saw as a boy was when I accompanied my father to one of the farms and I saw a bull mating. While my father did not want me to watch, I was still able to sneak a peak. Oh, what a sight that was for a young boy's eyes.

When the day was done, and if I required a bath, my mother would fill a large tub in the kitchen with hot water, and that is how I would clean myself up. All in all, my parents did everything humanly possible not only to provide for my needs, but to show me more love than any one boy could ever want or need.

CHAPTER 4

The Only One Smiling: Changes

"I was loved as much as any boy could have been loved."

By the time Alex was enrolled in kindergarten at the Catholic school in the town of Haltern am See, the influence of the Nazis was already being felt. Children were being indoctrinated and were already growing sullen. A picture of the kindergarten class of 1933 reveals Nazi flags in the background, and all of the children maintaining a somber demeanor – with the exception of one child. This child had curly brown hair and sat in the middle of the second row, intent on mugging a huge smile for the camera. He was, of course, Alex.

Alex first encountered the dreaded "Juden Verboten" or "Nicht fur Juden" signs in 1936 and 1937, primarily on most of the public buildings, as well as the "Kauf nicht bei Juden" (do not buy from Jews) and other swastika-filled graffiti on the Danielhaus, a millinery and haberdashery store, which was across from the old city hall and operated by a local Jewish family..

But it was not only in Haltern that Jews were being exposed to this treatment. Signs that said "Juden sind hier unerwunscht" ("Jews are *unwanted here") could be observed throughout Germany. However, in an effort to maintain the façade of goodwill and conceal any outward signs of anti-Semitism for the International Olympics of 1936, held in Berlin, Hitler had all such signs, in and around the Olympic venue, removed for the duration of the Games. When the Games were over, and the international community had left, the signs were quickly restored, and the efforts to push the Jews out of the Nazi sphere of influence were intensified.*

I knew that I was different from the time I went to kindergarten. I was always relegated to the back row of the classroom. When it came time to play, I would often be subjected to name calling, and on occasion, I would get into fights.

How can I possibly not remember what happened in 1934 when I was in first grade, less than seven years old, and the only Jewish kid in the class? I was accosted by fellow students while on the way home. As innocent and trusting as I was, I needed to learn quickly how to defend myself. This was when I first really understood that I was different from others. By the time I was in the first couple of grades beyond kindergarten, there was many a day that I would have to hide in one of the churches between school and my home, because there would be a gang of boys intent on beating me. This continued especially after *Kristallnacht*, when my only chance to attend a school was out of town, with the other Jewish children in the larger neighboring city of Recklinghausen. I would have to travel by train in order to go there, and quite often I would have to vary the train that I took by catching either an earlier or later one, because I knew that if I had taken my regularly-scheduled train there would be a gang of boys waiting to harass me, intimidate me by pushing me around, and on occasion, draw me into a fight. Once in a while they would go so far as to administer a beating to me. For this reason, I was always ready to defend myself.

It seems like only yesterday, and not 1935, when at age eight, I was excused to go home at midday while the children that remained in school had their Catholicism lessons. When I came back in the afternoon I would be shunned, and I remember how it depressed me. Weren't these the same children I had played with earlier in the morning in the schoolyard? What could have happened to have caused such a change? I couldn't understand it. Obviously, it was while I was dismissed from class to go home for religious lessons, that the other children in my Roman Catholic school would get the brainwashing lessons about Hitler and the Nazis. Even as early as kindergarten they were being exposed to it. Maybe if my parents had been more forthcoming and not so intent on shielding me from the harsh realities of the times, I would have comprehended it all that much more.

There was some name-calling, even back in 1936, with some reference to religion, but usually it was something like *"Judische schweinehund"* (Jewish pig dog), or even "dirty Jew" but I really was not aware of the persecution that was happening to the Jews. I mean, even if I was sometimes called a "dirty Jew," in all likelihood the kid who would call me that would also be the one who would come calling at my house if they needed a goalie for the soccer team. It really was a crazy time.

It was in 1937 when some of our neighbors who had children my age came to my house and talked to my parents and told them in no uncertain terms that they could not allow me to play with their children any more. While it may have been out of fear or even some of their own prejudice, eventually all of them would come around to that way of thinking. They actually went so far as to tell my parents that they would hold them responsible if I came to their houses looking for their children. Yet, even after that happened, some of the kids would come knocking on our door, especially if they were short a [soccer] goalie or something and ask, "Is Alexander here and does he want to play?" I would naturally want to go and play, but my parents would not allow me to do so for fear of the consequences. Sadly, my parents never really explained <u>why</u> I was not allowed to play with these boys and would simply say that I could not play with them any more. They would reassure me that I had not done anything wrong, but that was the extent of their explanation.

Soccer was obviously a passion for all of the boys that I grew up with at that time. One day, when I was about eight or nine years old and still permitted to play with the other non-Jewish boys, we were playing on one of the soccer fields on the outskirts of town down near the river. The three fields were actually tiered, with the lowest field being very near the river. This meant that when it rained, one or more of the fields might not be playable. The team from the local college, actually a semi-pro team, wanted to practice and tried to toss us off the only field that was dry enough. We put up a fuss and gave them all the "attitude" some eight and nine year olds could muster. Neither side was willing to leave, so we finally agreed that the winner of a free kick contest from the far line would retain the use of the field. As the goalie, I went into the net, and I was very much on guard, and ready. I was watching the huge kicker, sizing him up and watching his approach, in an effort to judge how he would angle his foot to kick the ball towards the net. I was really ready. I was in the zone. Nothing was going to get past me. Then he started moving towards the ball, only three or four meters. He didn't even take advantage of a full running start. And he kicked. And I was on it. I saw it the whole way. This rocket was coming straight at me. I jumped up, to meet the ball. And the ball, with me in front of it, slammed into the net. Goal for the other team. To this day, I would swear that it broke several of my ribs. That ball was kicked so hard that it was enough to lift me off of my feet, take my breath away, and send me flying into the net. I can still feel it. A pyrrhic victory of sorts: I had stopped the ball, but still surrendered the goal. We later found out that these guys were from the highest championship team, known as *Schalke 04*, a college from near Gelsenkirchen. It is now actually a full college that boasts a huge modern retractable dome stadium, worthy of a championship team which they truly were then, and continue to be to this day.

I also remember going with my mother to her hometown of Jever, where in addition to being with her people, I also experienced eating shrimp, still in the skins, for the first time. This was evidence that my mother was "cheating" on eating strictly kosher. They would actually sell these tiny shrimp from boiling pots of sea water on the street corner much like an American hot dog vendor. In a newspaper funnel they would be handed to us, and we would twist the tails off before we popped them in our mouths. My mother told me that they were a form of dried peas and beans that were peculiar to her town. In reality, it was another one of life's delicacies of which my mother was quite fond, and had acquired a taste for as a young girl. By telling me what she did, when we would return home and my father would ask me what I had eaten, I reported about the dried beans and all was well. He never found out. It was another secret that I shared with my dear mother.

I also remember that my mother's brother Karl Max Josephs had a large coffee roasting factory in Bremen and was in a position to provide my mother with coffee beans that she could make use of in helping supplement our family's income. She used to keep coffee on a high shelf over the stove, and after my father had lost his license and largely his livelihood, she would peddle these especially high quality roasted beans to our neighbors and other customers. Jews were still allowed to be peddlers, and out of respect for both my mother and my father, a lot of the non-Jews in town would buy my mother's coffee.

Because my father had lost his license and his ability to earn a living, it became increasingly difficult to support the entire family. At the same time, the laws had been changed forbidding Jews from hiring non-Jews to work for them in their homes. So, in an effort to ease the burden on our own household, as well as to present better opportunities to my sisters, my parents arranged for Rose to work in the household of a Jewish family in Oelde. This was short lived when the son in the house attempted to rape her. My parents saw to it that she got out of there. My other sister Alice went to work in Bielefeld, a town nearby, for another Jewish family. Alice was then in a position to help Rose find a new job in Bielefeld. This was also where Rose would meet her future husband, Edward Spanier. By 1939, shortly after *Kristallnacht*, my sisters, now 18 and 20 years of age, had immigrated to England. In time, both would end up in the United States.

The other advantage that my father was seeking for both of my sisters by having them go to work for other wealthy Jewish families was the assistance that these families could in turn provide to them. This is an example of Jews helping Jews.

I think it was because my parents were such good Germans that they naively clung to the belief that all the trouble being experienced by Jews and non-Jews alike would all blow over. While it may have been a certain amount of naiveté, I think it was also the fact that we lived a fairly sheltered life in Haltern, and because my parents maintained close relationships with all of our neighbors and the townspeople that had frequented my father's butcher shop over the years. I think it was a combination of this naiveté and a desire to always shield and protect me that kept me completely oblivious to what was going on around me until that horrible night of *Kristallnacht*. It was also this gullibility that prevented them from sending me on a *Kindertransport* to a safer place, especially after my older sisters had immigrated to England.

I was fortunate enough to have had two dogs while I was growing up. Herta was a black sheepdog and the other a Great Dane. Herta was playful and was a very good dog. I always enjoyed playing with her. She died of old age, and I was very sad, but at least I still had my Great Dane. When I was seven years old, I went into the barn one day to discover that the Great Dane had died. Sadly, by the time I had found him other animals had already begun to take pieces of him. This made the loss that much more traumatic and I cried a great deal. It was probably the worst thing that happened to me, which all in all, meant that I had enjoyed a pretty good childhood. It certainly paled in comparison to all the things I was to see in my teens as I survived camp after camp.

The *Danielhaus* also served as the Jewish Community Center. When the Jewish community was larger, one of the rooms in the center had been a classroom for Jewish school children. The entire building, the store and the residential portion, was owned by the Jewish community. It was located directly in front of the synagogue with a courtyard between them.

It was in this place that I learned more of the realities that my father and mother were facing as they lost their livelihood and began to lose their freedoms as well.

I remember an incident that took place either in front of our own house and butcher shop or in front of the *Danielhaus*. There were three guys, Brownshirts, who were carrying signs that discouraged people from doing business with Jews, and proclaimed that "Jews are our downfall." When I approached them, they said something like, "*Judische schweinehund gehen fester*" ("Jewish pig dog, move faster"), and then kicked me in the *tush* to put some emphasis on their command, which caused me to run inside. To this day, I just can't remember which building I was entering. I also remember coming home on occasion and finding things spray-painted on our front door, such as skull and crossbones, or "*Juden*" as well as other threatening messages. These were all efforts designed to drive the Jews out of Germany of their own volition, and was part of the entire program of excessive taxation, property seizure, and human degradation.

We were ordered to wear the yellow Star of David sewn to the front and back of our clothing, and to walk in the gutter of the street at this time as well. To say the least, this was very confusing to me. I could not comprehend why we had to change the manner in which we had lived my entire life.

CHAPTER 5

Dry Leaves

"The sound of dry leaves still frightens me to this day."

The two days of November 9 and 10, 1938 have come to be known historically as Kristallnacht, or Crystal Night: The Night of Broken Glass. It is perhaps the most terrifying two days of the entire seven year odyssey that Alex Lebenstein endured while the world went up in flames around him. Although many of the horrible memories of death and suffering have withdrawn to the outer recesses of his mind and soul, these are the two days and nights of terror that never leave, and that continue to haunt him even now, in his eighty first year. They provide the sounds and smells that to this day can still frighten this large powerful man.

Anti-Semitism did not start with Adolf Hitler and the rise of National Socialism; it had actually been a part of European life for a great number of years. As much a racial issue as a religious or social one, Jews became the scapegoats for all of Germany's problems, most of which stemmed from the Treaty of Versailles and the formal end to their defeat in World War I. Hitler merely used the Jews and the venom of hate to unify an otherwise frustrated and financially depressed people to consolidate his power.

At the time that Adolf Hitler consolidated his rise to power with his appointment to the office of Chancellor of Germany in January, 1933, there were approximately 568,000 living within the borders of Germany or less than 1% of a total population of 65 million inhabitants[2].Beginning in 1935, the government passed legislation, most notably, the Nuremberg Laws, which served to strip German Jews of their citizenship and isolate them by forbidding marriages between Jews and other citizens in Germany. By early 1939, approximately 225,000 Jews managed to muster the courage to abandon homes and businesses many had lived in for generations, and to immigrate to other countries.

In 1938, at the time of the Anschluss, or annexation of Austria into the German Reich, there were approximately 190,000 Jews living amidst the 4,800,000 people of Austria, or approximately 4% of the total population. This was already dramatically down from the 250,000 that had lived there a mere five years before. Many were professionals such as doctors, lawyers, bankers, engineers, and included the famed psychoanalyst Sigmund Freud who resided in Vienna, until his own forced emigration to London, England.

Perhaps the largest problem associated with the annexation of Austria was that it increased the size of the total Jewish population already living under the totalitarian regime of the Nazi party. Forced emigration had worked fairly successfully in Germany and was intensified in Austria. Leading the effort to deal with the Jewish problem was the soon to be infamous Adolf Eichmann. He would later be captured by Israeli agents in 1960 while living in Argentina and taken back to Israel for trial and subsequent execution.

It was in the spring of 1938 that this ambitious and zealous follower of Hitler began a campaign of terror that was intended to raise the desire of Austrian Jews to emigrate out of the Nazi sphere of influence. Excessive taxes were imposed; property was confiscated; licenses were revoked and bank accounts seized. The Austrian Jews were then presented with the choice of either internment in concentration camps or a passport marked with a giant 'J' [for Jew] for purposes of emigration out of the Reich. Those with both vision and the means to travel left their native land.

Unfortunately, the possession of a passport did not solve the problem for most European Jews. Despite the desire to address this issue with an international conference convened at the behest of U.S. President Franklin

D. Roosevelt, none of the countries that participated in the conference, with the exception of the Dominican Republic, were willing to open their borders and accept additional refugees. The Foreign Ministers of both France and Poland were two of the more outspoken representatives who convened at the French resort town of Evian-les-Bains on Lake Geneva, near the Swiss border, on July 6-15, 1938. All who gathered wanted to deal with their own Jewish problem and were therefore unwilling to accept any more Jews from areas controlled by Hitler's Third Reich. This reaction, along with the lack of outrage from the world following the Anschluss into Austria, further empowered Hitler to look for additional Lebensraum (living space) for the Germany Volk with the annexation of the Sudetenland (Czechoslovakia) in September 1938 and March 1939. In essence, to be a Jew was to be without a country. This response from the international community served only to confirm for Hitler that the world did not care about the plight of the Jew, and that he would be free to deal with the Jewish problem as he saw fit.

The annexation of the Sudetenland and its 3.5 million people also meant an additional 356,000 Jews in the Nazi sphere of influence, and served to reinforce Hitler's resolve to deal with this problem once and for all.

During 1938-39, in a program known as the Kindertransport, Britain admitted 10,000 unaccompanied Jewish children on an emergency basis. It was during 1939 that the United States received over 310,000 applications from German, Austrian, and Czech Jews for the 27,000 person quota for immigration by people of these nationalities.

From 1933 to 1938, Hitler and the National Socialist Party paid to the churches of Germany annual stipends ranging from 130 million to 500 million Reichsmarks[3]. This was in addition to the 85 million Reichsmarks being paid to the churches from the various states. The purpose was to encourage anti-Semitic remarks from the pulpits. The end result of this sponsorship was that the priest no longer had to do any fund-raising to support his parish, but it placed him under the control of the Nazi regime. With the commencement of formal hostilities and the enactment of steps towards the Final Solution, this support ceased, as did a tolerance for the preaching of religion and the mentioning of God in any manner; and the tide turned against the churches as well.

In early April, 1938, the Polish Parliament enacted legislation that revoked the citizenship of Poles, particularly Jews, who were then living abroad, unless they would return to Poland by November 1, 1938. Most of the Polish Jews residing in Germany were unwilling to return, and they ignored the law expecting no further repercussions. The Nazis, taking advantage of the November 1 deadline, expelled the Polish Jews from their homes. They were driven toward the border with only their basic belongings. Their properties and businesses were confiscated.

Poland however refused these native Jews re-entry into the country. The result was that a great number of Polish Jews ended up in a concentration camp near the border town of Zbaszyn. One such family was the Grynszpan family who had previously been living and prospering in the town of Hannover, Germany.

Herschel Greenspan (Grynszpan), then a 17 year old student studying in Paris, France, did not understand what his family could have done to warrant their forced removal from Germany or their incarceration in a concentration camp at the border between Germany and Poland. With only limited details of this harsh and nearly incomprehensible treatment of his family being provided by his sister Berta, he reacted with the outrage and zeal of a teenager and went to the German Embassy in Paris, on November 7, 1938. Upon entry into the embassy, he mortally wounded Ernst vom Rath, the Embassy's Third Secretary, who died two days later.

Hitler's Propaganda Minister, Joseph Goebbels, used this assassination as the catalyst for what would ultimately become the Final Solution in dealing with the Jewish Problem throughout Europe. In a program that was deemed as retribution for the assassination of vom Rath, the seeds of Kristallnacht were sown. Orders were sent out across Germany that "actions were to be taken against all Jews." These actions sanctioned the burning of synagogues, the looting of stores, businesses and homes owned and operated by Jews, as well as the terrorizing and degrading of the Jewish population.

In the course of Kristallnacht, Jews were beaten, some 91 killed, and over 27,000 arrested and taken to concentration camps, with the vast majority of the remaining Jewish population being forced to thereafter live in Jewish ghettos established within certain towns.

A fine of one billion Reichsmarks (about $400 million in 1938) was imposed on the Jewish community for vom Rath's death[4]. Insurance payments for damage caused by the attacks of November 9 and 10, totaling some 25 million Reichsmarks, were also confiscated, thus leaving Jewish shop owners the additional financial burden of rebuilding, if that was possible at all.

With the advent of the activities of those fateful two days in November, life for the German Jew would never be as it had been. Gone were the days when a Jew could live in harmony with his Christian neighbor; sharing the spirit of Christmas and the traditions of the Passover; or enjoy a game of soccer regardless of nationality or religion.

By the time of Kristallnacht, the Jewish population of Haltern had shrunk from the approximately forty families of 1933, to a mere twenty families. The 12,000 residents of this small town [and 36,000 in the greater Haltern area] lived in the relative harmony previously described. The bonds between them, Jew and non-Jew, had largely been forged on the battlefields of France, when Natan Lebenstein, a devout German Jew had answered the call of the Fatherland and gone off to war with his Aryan friends. This wartime experience had taken mere friends and acquaintances and created the unbreakable bonds of a brotherhood forged in the fires of War.

While reports of the synagogues being burned in Munich in June, and in Nuremberg in August of 1938 had reached the good people of Haltern, the reality and gravity of the situation clearly had not. Many residents, including Natan and Lotte Lebenstein, their eleven year old son Alex, as well as their Jewish and non-Jewish friends, simply did not believe that the destruction that Nazi groups were inflicting on the rest of the country would reach the tranquility of their town. But then it happened, shattering their beliefs to the contrary.

In the beginning of the 20th Century, anti-Semitism increased dramatically in Eastern Europe. After the First World War, masses of mostly Orthodox Jews came into Germany to escape persecution in other countries. Germany needed to be rebuilt, anti-Semitism was not as prevalent, and they saw an opportunity to make a life there. But then it was not uncommon to have Jews fighting among themselves. You would have a Polish or other Eastern European Jew peddling his wares from a pushcart that he operated in front of a German Jew's store. The store owner, who was more fully assimilated, had developed his own clientele over the years and was naturally angry; these confrontations often led to violence. The Eastern European Jews, who were more often Orthodox in religious practice, dress, and appearance, really stood out. This tended to make the German Jew ashamed of being associated with this sect, or at the very least, be put in a very awkward position. There were no Jewish department stores in our modest town. The Orthodox Jewish peddlers from the East went to larger cities, so we never experienced a confrontation, and I only learned about this later.

Everyone, to include my parents and their friends, Jews and non-Jews alike, dismissed Hitler, as others like him, until it was too late.

It was the morning of November 9th, and many of the people that knew and respected my parents began to come to reassure us that we would surely be in no danger from the craziness and destruction that Jews were suffering in other cities across the country.

"Natan, you are such a good German, surely no harm will come to you or your family," said one of his Christian friends, and my father wanted to believe.

"Natan, what we have heard on the radio that is happening to the Jews is only happening in the big cities. Berlin, Dortmund, and Essen -- the big cities where there are lots of wealthy Jews. Things have been good here, and surely you will all be safe in Haltern," said another friend, with great pain in his voice. And my father wanted to believe. We were forced to rely on our neighbors for the news that they heard on the radio because we, like all Jews, were forbidden to own a radio. This prohibition had existed since the same time that all Jews lost their business licenses. It was yet one more way to degrade us.

"Natan, it won't happen here, and you and your family will be okay. It is obvious that the Nazis are after the money, and that is why they are in the big cities with this nonsense. They are only going after the rich Jews," encouraged yet another good Christian friend, and my father began to believe what these loyal friends and neighbors were saying to him.

Morning passed into afternoon, and afternoon into evening. More friends continued to come by to press reassurances upon my father, until the darkness of night came. And still, the cobblestoned streets remained quiet, and my father and mother quietly, albeit cautiously, rejoiced. Perhaps we would be spared after all. Though I was only a week past my eleventh birthday, I remained aware and nervous, but my parents reassured me. Still very much my Mama's boy, I stayed close to her, finding comfort in the warmth of our kitchen, as I watched my mother cook our dinner, as well as receiving reassurance from her that life as we knew it would continue for us in Haltern. We ate dinner that night, with gratitude in our hearts, and I remember crawling into my parents' bed exhausted and frightened. I was sleeping there between them because they wanted me close, and I freely admit I wanted to be there too. Looking back, I can understand why.

The peace of mind with which we slept on the night of November 9 was quickly shattered when more of my parents' friends returned on the morning of November 10. The confidence with which they had spoken to my father only the day before, as they reassured their Jewish friend, was not as great the morning of this day; for all had been listening to the reports being passed by word of mouth and over the primitive radio of that time. The news was not good, and it was becoming apparent that the terror that had been inflicted on the Jews in the larger cities across Germany would quickly become a living nightmare in the smaller towns such as Haltern.

"Natan, you are a good German. You served Germany and you were decorated in the war. They will respect you and your family. No harm will befall you," said one of my father's former war comrades.

As the hours passed, we received more and more news of the horrible activities taking place in cities and towns closer and closer to us. Yet, my father still nervously believed. At age fifty eight, having lost his license as a Master Butcher several years earlier, his sole concern now was the safety of my mother and me.

At ten o'clock in the morning we received word that they had destroyed and plundered the home of Abraham Weyl, the only rich Jew who lived in Haltern. His home was several blocks away from our own.

"You see, Natan. They are only going after the rich Jews," said one of my father's friends in an attempt to continue the charade. We then heard reports of the next house being destroyed. Then it was the Herzberg house. And then Herman Cohen's house was pillaged and looted as well, and I could feel the tension building in the air, as if a storm were approaching us.

One of my father's friends continued to attempt to reassure him and pointed out that we were not wealthy people, and that surely we would be spared for that reason alone.

At three o'clock in the afternoon, the synagogue in which we had worshipped for generations was desecrated; books, Torah scrolls, and the balance of the interior were being burned or destroyed in the street for all to see. I was more scared than I had been in my entire life.

"Natan, we will stay with you. You are a loyal German. You fought bravely with many of us in the War. Go, put on your medals, and they will see that you are a loyal German who faithfully served the Fatherland. They won't hurt you," said one of my father's friends, attempting to be helpful and reassuring. With this bit of wishful thinking, my father went into our house and pinned his medals to his jacket, believing that the forces of evil could still be blunted by the evidence of his faithful service as a German soldier. He went back outside to stand with his friends and neighbors, proudly wearing his medals, still wanting to believe, and looking very much like the hero he had always been to me.

As we stood there outside our home, I put my hand in my father's as I often did. For my entire life, my father had been my hero because he was always so physically strong and so brave; so respected by the community that he served and lived within; so capable, and such a tower of confidence. Today, however, I experienced something that I had never felt before. I felt perspiration on my father's hands. It became clear to me that he too was very nervous. This fact alone was enough to frighten me even more.

We could hear the roar of an angry crowd coming towards us from the neighboring blocks on which the synagogue and the homes of other Jews had been ransacked and destroyed.

Another friend came to us in advance of the mob to warn us that Nazis from out of town had come to stir up and organize some of the local Party members. With tears and genuine fear for us, he quietly brought us this warning.

It takes about ten times as long to describe the most terrifying events of *Kristallnacht* than it did for the events of that day to take place, for they happened bang, bang, bang.

The mob rapidly came closer and closer. They were shouting many of the horrible anti-Semitic things that had been printed in *Der Sturmer*, a newspaper that had long published caricatures and other degrading pictures of Jews, as well as many hateful lies about things that Jews were purported to have done. I had little knowledge of these things, or at the very least, did not understand them. I had been so sheltered by my parents and shielded from the realities of that time. Most of what I had encountered until now seemed more like the same, sometimes mean and hateful, playground antics of children. But this, I knew, was something far more than that. I could hear the crowd coming towards our house, and I felt the icy tentacles of utter fear gripping my heart.

They were making terrible noise as they came closer to our house. As they drew nearer, I could see that they were armed with axes and crowbars, cattle prods, tree limbs, broom sticks, and clubs. Others carried rocks and stones to be thrown at us as well as through our windows. Leading the way in front of the Brownshirts of the SA was a group of boys my own age, boys that I knew and with whom I had attended kindergarten and the first three years of [Catholic] elementary school, or shared soccer fields with here in Haltern. They too were armed with stones and sticks and slingshots and they all came directly at me. I wanted to shout at them to stop and to tell them that they can't do this to my family, but I had no voice. The words would not come out of my throat. All I could do was to stand there and wonder what I had done to receive such punishment and degradation. At my young age, I could not even begin to fathom or grasp it. To this day, I am nothing short of amazed that I survived the day. They continued to shout horrible words at us and threw things at me, shooting rocks and stones with their slingshots. Each of these missiles hurt me physically, but wounded my heart and soul far more deeply. They are very much wounds that I still feel to this day.

My father stood proudly in front of the rabble pleading with many who were life-long acquaintances and cried out, "You cannot do this to me! I am a German like you." He was gesturing with his arms, patting his chest to draw attention to his medals, as if to make this hate-filled Nazi crowd recall his own loyalty as well as the hardships they had mutually endured in France twenty years earlier.

Seemingly in the blink of an eye, the crowd parted, and the Nazi, who was in charge of the horrible things that were happening in Haltern that day, came up to my father, got very close to him, began to shake him violently by the shoulders, and then spat in his face. All the while my father was protesting what was happening and proclaiming that he was a good and loyal German, this officer was shouting at my father, and then began to beat him. It was while he was beating my father, that he yelled, "You are not a German. You are a dirty Jew. You are not human, and you do not deserve to wear these medals," and ripped my father's medals from his chest and threw them to the ground. To further make his twisted point, he stomped on those revered pieces of ribbon and metal, grinding them into the cobblestones under the heel of his black leather jackboots, and kicked them toward a blazing fire in the street.

At the same time that this was going on, many in the crowd had roughly surged passed us and quickly entered our house and shop, and threw furniture and other of our belongings out on to the street through the windows. They were looting the place of our valuables and we heard my mother, defenseless, in the house, screaming in pain, while she too was being beaten; "Natan, Alex! Let's get out of here…let's get out of here! They are killing us! They are killing us!" My father grabbed me by the neck and propelled me into the house to my mother's side. I grew more terrified with each passing moment.

As I reached my mother, my father grabbed both of us, and with his strong arms propelled us through and out of the house. I am not sure how we were able to do so, but we escaped, all the way to the back of our property. And there we stood, in the *Wehrstrasse (alley)*, watching them destroy all that my father and my grandfather before him had worked lifetimes to build.

We stood there nursing our wounds. The physical ones were bleeding and eventually healed. But the far more painful mental and emotional scars will never leave me. We were trying to catch our breath and wondering what would become of us. None of us spoke for a long time. There were no words that could adequately convey what each of us was feeling at that time. As we stood there we could still hear the screaming hordes that were looting and destroying our home; the sounds of breaking glass, and the thud of our furniture landing in the street. Through it all, there was always the sound of the wind blowing.

After what seemed like hours, but was probably only minutes, my mother asked my father, "Natan, what are we going to do now?"

"Let's wait a while, and when things have quieted down, we'll go back and we'll bring the furniture into the house, save what we can, and things will be better," he replied.

As the crowd finished plundering our home, several of my father's friends came to us as we leaned against the picket fence at the rear of our property, and pleaded with my father to leave. "Natan, you can't stay here. We are powerless to protect you. If they find you here, they will beat you again. There is no controlling them. You must go and take your family away from here and go to a safer place."

My father asked, "Leave here? Where to? Where should I go with my wife and son to be safe?"

His friends interrupted him and suggested that for our own protection, we should go the short distance down the *Garden Strasse* to our garden, if for no other reason than to get away from the crowd that was certainly intent on terrorizing us as well as all of the other Jews in town that day. We would probably be safer there, and we could wait for things to quiet down, and for people to come back to their senses. Like most German families of this time, mine had a very large garden where we would grow vegetables and fruits which my mother would then can and preserve for us to eat in the winter. While the entire family was responsible for planting, weeding, and tending the garden, my contributions usually consisted of sitting there and eating the fruits of our labors. There were no supermarkets back then, and these gardening and canning activities were something that a family did in order to survive the winter.

We made our way the quarter mile to our garden. Luckily, *Garden Strasse* and the dormant gardens were deserted. The primitive gazebo in our garden where my father used to play cards with his friends gave us some protection from the approaching night. During the growing seasons, the sides and trellis of the gazebo would be covered with the beans that grew up towards the sun before we would pick them. There were no beans left in November, just the empty dry vines and leaves that eerily danced in the wind. They scraped themselves against the wooden beams every time the wind would blow, creating an empty sound that still sends chills up and down my spine to this very day. Of all the sights and sounds that left a lasting impression on me during the years that I fought to survive, there is no doubt that the sounds I experienced while we huddled on the gazebo are the ones that will forever haunt me. Even now, I cannot hear the sound of leaves scraping on the sidewalk or the bricks of my apartment without flashing back to the time that we huddled on that old gazebo and that eerie sound of dead leaves and vines added to the sheer terror that I was feeling.

It was now about four-thirty in the afternoon on that chilly gray day. The wind was blowing, and we were cold. Our friends returned just before dark, bringing us blankets, coffee, and some soup to help us keep warm. One of my father's best friends soon came riding as fast as he possibly could into the garden on his bicycle, obviously alarmed. He jumped off the bike even before he had used the brakes to stop it, allowing the bike to go on without him. Greatly agitated, he stormed into the garden and yelled, "Natan, it is not safe for you to stay here. We must find a better place for you. I just heard a rumor that the Nazi who attacked you when they came to destroy your home, the one who spat in your face, beat you, and ripped off your medals, is claiming that you spat into his face and hit him. But worse than that, his superior officer told him that the medals you were wearing should have been turned in two and a half years ago. Did you know that all Jewish soldiers were required to turn in their medals two and a half years ago? Obviously, you didn't do that, and others who defied this law were never heard from again. This Nazi is looking for you."

"Where can I go? Everyone here knows me. I have no way to leave. No horse and buggy, no bicycle. People will recognize me. Where shall I go?" pleaded my father, stunned and looking to heaven, as if seeking advice from God. There was a moment of quiet. He then turned to my mother and said, "Lotte, I'm going to give myself up. Then maybe no harm will come to you and Alex."

Another friend, hearing my father utter these words, raised his fist and got so mad at him that I thought he might beat my father. He yelled, "Natan, how dare you talk like this! That is not what you should do! You have always been brave, and have never given up on anything at any time in your life. You are the head of your family. You can't leave them during this horrible time. You must stay with them. You must leave this garden and find another place to hide until things calm down here."

"So give me an idea," said my father. "What can we do? Where can I go?"

"Go to the Jewish cemetery; they will not look for you there," said another of his friends, referring to the cemetery located on the outskirts of our town.

"Yes, Natan, go to the cemetery. There is nothing for them to steal or to plunder out there," said another friend. "Surely you will be safe there."

"But people will see us as we walk through the town," reasoned my father.

"No they won't, Natan. They are all too busy looting and stealing from you and the other Jewish families. No one will find you in the cemetery. Be patient. We will come back for you when it is safe for you to leave."

Taking our blankets, we trudged through the cold, damp darkening air. Being November, the weather had already turned cold, and much like Upstate New York, the air had an edge that was nothing less than bone chilling when the wind blew. We quietly walked to the cemetery and approached a sloping ravine in the back of the property. At the far end, it was some eight to ten feet deep, and by hunkering down inside of it, we were somewhat protected from the wind. We huddled there for a long time. Of course, I had never been in a cemetery at night. The silence was extremely frightening. No birds were singing, and the darkness felt darker than any I had ever known before. Once in a while, the silence was broken by the wind in the trees and dry leaves scraping against the headstones. Hours passed, I don't know how many, because I was too frightened to even be aware of time passing. Just yesterday I had been sitting in the warmth of our kitchen watching my mother fix our dinner, living a seemingly normal life, and today I was huddling in the wind having seen my father beaten and our life destroyed because we were now deemed to be something less than human. But for the moment, we felt safe.

We were shocked and surprised when the quiet of the dark night was suddenly shattered by the noise of the approaching mob. Still armed with the axes and crowbars, now many of them were holding kerosene lamps with large wicks that served to light up the way around them, casting an evil and eerie glow, and allowing me to see their breath in the cold night air. Still shouting their obscene slogans, they had come to the cemetery after all.

"Someone must have sold us out and revealed our location to the mob," said my mother, now very frightened. From our vantage point, we knew when they entered because of the squeak of the gate at the cemetery entrance which had not been oiled in years. That particular squeak also remains in my head to this day. Then we heard the cracking of concrete and marble as they began to destroy the headstones with German and Hebrew inscriptions, even taking out their hatred on the dead.

"We are certainly in the right place. We won't ever leave here," my mother softly whispered amidst her tears, as I clung to her.

"Shh," instructed my father, as he put his strong arms around us.

We sat there, frozen in fear, listening to them destroying the headstones, axes and crowbars striking and shattering them, sending shards of stone flying in all directions. These wild men and boys kept shouting, and to our minds looking for us as well. It took them about an hour to destroy the cemetery. Just when we thought that they might be finished, we heard the distinct sounds of shovels striking the earth and digging going on.

"They are digging our graves," softly cried my mother. "They know that we are here," she said, drawing me closer.

"Lotte," said my father in an attempt to quiet her.

"They are saving us for last," said my mother, resignation in her voice.

While at age eleven I did not really understand death, having been only five years old when my older sister departed this life, the fear in my mother's voice was enough to make my increasing fear almost too much to bear.

Between the curiosities that were driving me, and in an effort to stay aware of what was going on, I would crawl up the edge of the ravine and look out from behind the tall dry grass. As I did this yet another time, I was shocked to see in the dim lantern light a very large Nazi in full uniform, starting to walk toward where we were hiding. My heart raced harder and faster as I slid back down. I thought my heart might even pop out of my chest. I could hear it beating in my chest and both feel and hear the blood pumping through my ears as well. I told my mother that someone was coming, and my father tightened his grip on my mother and me. Then there was silence and we held our breath.

The silence was broken by approaching footsteps as they appeared to be coming closer to us as we could hear the crunching grass and twigs. The footsteps suddenly stopped, and we were left to wonder what was happening.

My curiosity and need for information once again drove me up to peek out from the top of the ravine to see what was going on. The Nazi officer was nearly on top of us. He kept looking around, and in my imagination, it was as if his eyes were search light beams looking for us. Looking around one more time, as if checking to see that nobody was looking he unzipped his pants and began to relieve his bladder in our direction. Because I had been raised so modestly, I averted my eyes, but I could still hear his urine spattering on the ground. When he was done, he zipped his pants, yelled something to the other men and turned and walked away. Shortly thereafter they left the cemetery. The blood and adrenalin that had been pumping so hard through my chest and head slowed down as quickly as it had sped up, leaving me weak in the knees and a bit lightheaded.

More time passed, and the cold had completely engulfed my body. I don't know if I slept at all, but we stayed in the cemetery for a long time. I was huddled between my mother and father as we attempted to find warmth from one another's bodies. I was so cold and so frightened that there was no saliva in my mouth, and no more tears to be shed. I simply clung to my mother, attempting to find some degree of comfort within this living nightmare.

As I was lying there, I listened to the wind blowing the dried leaves amidst the rubble of the now-destroyed headstones and the rustling of the empty tree branches. I can't remember what went through my mind. It certainly seemed as if our lives would soon be over. All of the things that my father's friends could never imagine happening here in Haltern had happened. Life as we knew it was surely over. I couldn't even imagine that there would be a tomorrow. What a horrible thought for an eleven-year-old boy to have, but that was what made that day so frightening, even as I think of it after the passage of seventy years.

It was probably about four o'clock in the morning when some of my father's friends returned and led us to the basement of an old hotel in town. It was the old Sondermann Hotel operated by Frau Anne Plum and her family. But for their courage and kindness I don't know what we would have done that night and in the days to come.

Little could I guess that this was merely the first chapter of the ordeals that would be coming my way in a very short span of time. It would have been hard for me to imagine that I would soon be living day to day; survival dependent upon my ability to ignore pain, fatigue, hunger, sickness, disease, beatings, and always, always, the degradation. None of the atrocities that I would witness or have inflicted upon me could measure up to the intense pain caused by the constant degradation. But we persevered and battled on, day by day. To have done otherwise would have meant death. You did not make an issue of any of these things, because to do so would be your downfall. Instead, we hurt, we cried, we bled inside out, and made this a routine that we followed each and every day. The way to win was to survive. It becomes an issue of mind over matter. Your body does not absolutely require three meals a day. I would start to find that out this very day.

Oh how wonderful it felt to walk into the warmth of the basement of the hotel, and to be out of the cold and the wind. I know I went to sleep curled up in a blanket in a corner, and I think my fatigue was due more to nervous exhaustion than anything else. Nonetheless, just being warm and protected from the elements was relief in itself. The food that we were fed never tasted so good. Maybe it was the kindness with which it was sprinkled.

It was while we were in the basement of the hotel that my father tried to reassure my mother and me, but he already knew that we would never be able to return to our home, and replace the furniture that had been thrown out into the street and to pretend that this had never happened. The time that we spent in the basement was really a time of consoling one another, and taking a reality check. By the time we left the basement, we knew that life was going to be completely different than it had ever been before. This was acceptance of a very harsh reality.

I think that for a long time after *Kristallnacht* my father was genuinely confused by the events that were taking place around him. Despite it all, he still considered himself a good German. I think he still harbored the naïve hope that things would blow over and that life as we had known it would be restored. It took a long time before his confusion turned into bitter, spirit-breaking disappointment.

Keeping in mind that we did not get to the hotel until nearly four o'clock in the morning, it was actually later that day and into the evening that we became painfully aware of the fact that the Nazi hoodlums were celebrating their victory over the Jews of Haltern by toasting one another with drinks and being loud and boisterous in the hotel's bar and dining room, which was directly over our heads.

Several days passed while we remained hidden in the basement of the hotel. The time we spent there allowed me to take a mental inventory of my feelings. We were warm, there was food to eat, and it seemed that things quieted down over the next few days. I continued to pester my mother about returning to our home. I am not certain if I was even aware of the risk that the people who assisted us had taken upon themselves, but I look back now and realize, that even amidst all the evil, that there were in fact good people. While one bad apple can indeed spoil the barrel, I am grateful for the number of good apples that I encountered in my odyssey to hell and back.

I have largely been able to cope with all the atrocities of the war that I witnessed with the exception of my experiences of *Kristallnacht* in front of my home and the events of the cemetery. To this day, they remain wounds that will neither heal nor allow me to forget. They presented themselves as the single largest obstacle to my returning to any form of a normal life. I realize today that the mental pain done to my inner self was far worse than any of the physical challenges that I encountered later in any of the camps.

The degradation was by far the worst part of this entire ordeal. Spirits were broken and lives completely disrupted, if not destroyed. I will never forget what it did to my own father and mother, or the manner in which it has scarred me to this day. With the systematic and ruthless tactics of these murderous dogs, it was very easy to quickly feel less than human and to ultimately lose the will to live. But as bad as all of this was, it would pale in comparison to what awaited us during our six day ordeal in the cattle cars.

PART II

Darkness

When Alex is in the schools talking to the children, he is often asked questions about the time that he spent in the camps, even though he does give a disclaimer very early in his presentation that it is not his intent to talk about the gruesome events and images of these times - especially since they can be so readily found in very graphic detail, in thousands of books, pictures, and movies. Between what the Nazis so carefully documented as their work in dealing with the Final Solution, and what the Allies did to both preserve it and to capture it in their own films and pictures, there can be no doubt that it occurred and that it was indeed the darkest hours of Man's modern history. As we probed Alex's memories, we were amazed at the manner in which these dark images had been so carefully compartmentalized in a mode of self defense. We had agreed early on that he would probe his memories this one last time and would attempt to dredge up as much of the darkness as he could, much as he had dredged up the dark wet soil in the peat bogs so many years ago while a prisoner in a slave labor camp. As we talked about the sights, the sounds, the smells, and all that he remembered about these dark years, our respect and love for him grew. To have witnessed it is one thing, to have survived it another. But to emerge from it not completely non-functioning emotionally and socially is nothing short of extraordinary.

As we have said before, Alex is a man of great warmth and passion, a bear of a man, who greets one and all that he knows with open arms and free kisses. Knowing now what he saw, smelled, and endured, makes the opportunity to write this book and to spend time with this man a precious privilege.

It has been some sixty plus years since I have thought about a number of the events that I witnessed or survived during the time that I was a teenager. I must refer to myself as a teenager, and can't say child, because I largely did not have a childhood after the evening of *Kristallnacht.* This dark period of my life was so traumatic that it is only recently that I have been able to confront the shadows and noises that still cause me to start whenever I see or hear them. As we wrote this book, chapter by chapter, sitting at the dining room table in my home, the tape recorder softly humming, I simply responding to questions that were put to me, I was sometimes overwhelmed, as was everyone at the table, by the emotions that came flooding back as I recalled the often tragic results of these different stories and anecdotes.

CHAPTER 6

Judenhaus: Muenster Strasse #28

"We were the last five to leave."

Within a few days of *Kristallnacht*, the City Elders knew where all the Jews were hiding. As part of their duties they were directed to establish a ghetto in which the Jews could live and continue to work. People often ask me if there was ever any resistance to the orders of the Nazis. Certainly there was, but disobedience usually was dealt with quite severely, and dissenters would often disappear never to be seen nor heard from again. I do not recall witnessing any resistance while living in the *Judenhaus*.

It was a few days later, and after the time that we had been relocated to the *Judenhaus* or miniature ghetto at *Muenster Strasse #28*. Actually the term "ghetto" would be an exaggeration in terms of the City of Haltern. We were living in a large loft in the house of Hermann Cohen.

This house, where all the Jews of Haltern would be forced to live, was approximately an eight minute walk from my old house. At first, many of the city's Jews were living there. My parents, an aunt, and I shared one of the rooms. For those fortunate enough to have means to leave, emigration meant escape from the ensuing madness. It also served to reduce the number of residents, and soon there was more space for those of us who remained there to spread out. This continued until there were only five of us left in the entire town.

Despite the relocation, I was still very naïve and did not realize that we did not have a house to return to, much less that we would never be allowed to do so. Adding to my confusion was the fact that we were allowed to walk to stores, so long as we did so with permission. It was during one of these designated times, when we were actually standing in front of our house at *Disselhof 36,* that I asked, "Momma, why don't we go back to our house?"

"Alex, we don't have a house anymore," is what she replied to me. I did not remember this exchange with my mother until I was reminded of it by Anna Boehmer in around the year 2002. At the time of that recollection, Anna was still residing in the City of Haltern and was a very alert 91 years of age. I also remember my mother walking up and down the sidewalk in front of our old house, looking between the cobblestones for any small item of value that may lay hidden. To the best of my recollection, we never found anything. I remember the sadness that this too brought to my mother.

I do remember, shortly after this conversation, that our house was re-occupied by another family. I would also presume that they did so after having purchased it from the bank that had held the mortgage on it. Likewise, our beloved garden, which was either confiscated or foreclosed upon, was no longer ours. I cannot describe the feeling that I had when I saw other people living in what I had always known to be our house. The new owner of the house was a trucker, because back in the yard where our livestock used to be was where he would keep and service his truck.

I have heard a story from one of my parents' neighbors, the Pillmans, that they actually kept a chest of my mother's silver, and whenever money was very low, my mother would go see Mrs. Pillman and take a piece or two that she would then sell or trade for food or other commodities. While I don't remember this, I think that it is probable that this happened.

My formal education, which now stood at three years, could be continued if I went to another town where there was a Jewish school, and so it was that I would take the train to Recklinghausen, where I was instructed by a man by the name of Eric Jacobs, who later came to the United States and ironically, became a kosher butcher. I would not be allowed to return to my class at the Catholic school in Haltern, even to sit in my seat in the very back of the room. My mother was correct when she had told me that our home was gone. Of course it really didn't matter, because all of the remaining Jews that we knew in the town were forced to live with us in the *Judenhaus*.

As a boy of eleven and the only child living in the house, I was left largely to my own devices. I would play by myself in the big backyard, kicking or bouncing a ball against the wall of the house. The wooden door could be used as a simulated goal in which to kick the ball, or I would just keep count of the number of times I could successfully hit a certain spot in the bricks. The wall was the opponent against whom I played. While I would occasionally see some of the other boys with whom I had played soccer, I was never allowed to play with them. Even if we had been willing, they were afraid to speak to me either because their parents were themselves afraid, or because they had been brainwashed. Of course, some of them were anti-Semitic by this time, and would spit on the ground in my direction, or even mumble 'dirty Jew' under their breath.

My religious education continued in Recklinghausen where I was able to read from a *Torah* (holy scrolls that constitute the first books of the Old Testament) that was otherwise kept hidden in a wall. The biggest challenge to worshipping back then was the ability to have a *minyan*, or the requisite ten men necessary to conduct services.

For quite a while, the City Elders in Haltern were able to protect those of us who were living in the *Judenhaus*. This was partly because there were so few of us and partly because of the good relationships that my father had enjoyed with many of these prominent city leaders, as well as the fact that the Nazis had bigger fish to fry in the larger cities and metropolitan areas.

It is with some degree of irony that I look back on our time in the *Judenhaus,* and I realize that we probably had more food during that time than most other Germans. My family was well liked and my father respected. The friendly relationships, both personal and business, that he had with the many farmers of the area certainly influenced these righteous people to come to our aid in our time of need. So, in addition to the food stamps that we were issued by the authorities, these good people were secretly supplying us with food. By doing so, they risked their very lives to come to our aid. It was not something lost on me, even then as a young boy.

At designated hours, usually after dark, we were permitted to go shopping and to use our allocation of food stamps, as long as we entered by way of the back door of the stores that we frequented. My recollection is that shop owners were afraid to have Jewish people in their stores during the day when they might be seen for fear of being accused of regularly selling to Jews, or worse, showing any kind of friendship to a Jew. To do so would raise suspicion and leave them vulnerable to questioning by the authorities. I remember shopping with my mother at Bertling's meat market, a store that my father had done business with in years past, and being grateful for what we could bring home. They were good to us and often would throw a little extra into our purchase.

My father was like a lost person by the time we entered the *Judenhaus*. Never a conversationalist, he was even more subdued than when I was younger. He had pretty much lost everything that he valued both monetarily and as a person. He had lost his business, but more importantly he had lost his identity as a proud German Jew. He had been a decorated war veteran and now he could not even take pride in that status. The Nazis were very successful in their efforts to degrade when it came to my father. He was very much a beaten man. The one bright spot was when he was finally permitted to work for a short while at the brick factory on the *Muenster Strasse*. While the work disillusioned him, it was far better than simply sitting in the *Judenhaus* all day long. I don't know how he was treated there, but I can only assume that it was not an entirely pleasant experience for him. He would ride a bicycle to work, and he would spend the day in the brick factory doing who knows what. I also remember that on the grounds of the brick factory there was a man-made pond from which years before the clay for the bricks had been drawn, and no more usable clay could be removed. It eventually became full of fish, and I would at times fish there in an effort to entertain myself.

My mother became far less emotional after the events of *Kristallnacht*. The effects of the entire ordeal were very evident in her. Due to the unavailability of coffee as well as the new laws that went into effect, she was no longer allowed to peddle the coffee as she had been doing to supplement our family's income, and she was largely left to sit in the *Judenhaus*, pondering our fate.

In 1939 and even later, it was still possible to in some cases to leave the country. As time went on, and the numbers of Jews residing in the *Judenhaus* dwindled, we became increasingly isolated. None of us were openly interacting with the rest of the town's people, again because of restrictions being placed on us, on them, and out of a general fear that affected all of us. Even those who were not ardent supporters of the Nazis were already "cooked" themselves, as individual freedoms continued to disappear.

It was in January, 1942, that the order came in for us to be relocated to a larger ghetto in Riga, Latvia. By this time, we had virtually no resources available to us. When an officer came to the house and told my father that the remaining five Jews were to be relocated, he then proceeded to count, "One, two, three, four, five. That will be two hundred and fifty *Reichsmarks* for the five of you to be relocated."

"How do you expect me to pay you two hundred and fifty *Reichsmarks*?" asked my father. "You can see that we have nothing."

"If you don't have sufficient means to pay, you will need to go to the City Hall and ask them for assistance," said the official.

My father in fact went to the City Hall, and there is, in the archives, a copy of the affidavit that my father signed on behalf of himself, my mother, me, as well as Herman Cohen and Frau Jenny Kleeberg, acknowledging our inability to pay for our own transportation to wherever the Nazis were sending us.

Years later, I was asked why we were the last ones to leave the city. Actually it is very clear to me as to why we were the last ones left. Some of it was because everyone else had left for larger towns (from where they may have been transported to a concentration camp), or to immigrate to other countries. My father's reputation in town was such that we were left alone until the time that this final order came down that the town must be made *Judenrein* or "Jew-free." If you were old, or appeared feeble, or you were too skinny, you would in all likelihood be sent off for extermination. By this time, Hermann Cohen was very old and in all likelihood died in a cattle car, or was earmarked for immediate extermination along with Jenny Kleeberg. In any event, I never laid eyes on either one of them when we arrived in Riga. I can only assume that they were never sent there. Because my parents and I were all healthy and strong and did not wear strong eyeglasses or have any other visible limps or physical disabilities, we were spared and sent to the ghetto in Riga. To my knowledge, nobody knew that they were leaving for any place remotely resembling a death camp. It was all part of the façade that the Nazis wanted to maintain.

CHAPTER 7

The Smell of Fear: In the Cattle Cars

"I actually had the best spot in the car..."

Much has been written about Benito Mussolini and the manner in which the Italian railroads always ran efficiently and on time, despite the constant change in government form and leadership. Likewise, the German railroad, or Reichsbahn, was very efficient. In fact, it played a very critical role in the Final Solution as it pertained to the Jews and other groups. The transportation of those not deemed desirable by the Nazis was yet another example of efficiency gone awry. Working with Adolf Eichmann and his henchmen, train officials organized Sonderzuge, or special trains, that collected Jews from all over Europe and transported them to places like Auschwitz, Birkenau, and Treblinka, just to name a few of the more prominently infamous death camps.

With nearly the commonality of some brand names that have come to be identified with specific products, such as Kleenex, the term cattle car has been used very readily over the past sixty years since the end of the war to describe the method of transportation for millions of Jews and other victims of the Holocaust. Hundreds and thousands of these railroad cars were utilized, and were specifically called cattle cars to further degrade and to dehumanize their victims. They were linked to locomotives, and used to transport Jews such as Alex and his family, under extremely adverse conditions, to places with names familiar and unfamiliar. But what did a cattle car actually look like? How big was it? After all, Jews were often charged a fare for relocation or transportation; under what conditions did they travel? Surely if they were being relocated for work or labor purposes and paying for the transportation, it must resemble something that we would all be familiar with today. No, in actuality, these victims of the Reich were transported in rough hewn wooden rail cars, built in the first ten to twelve years of the 20th Century. Built with no seats, no benches, no heat, no light, no food, no sanitation facilities, they were in fact originally designed to transport cattle being sent to the slaughterhouses of Europe. In a space measuring only 31 x 13, as many as eighty to one hundred people, mainly Jews, would be packed in, tightly, with no idea of how long they would have to endure these conditions. For this reason, people often went mad. Spirits broke. Old people died. Babies cried until they died.

For Alex and his parents, the cattle car mode of transportation involved their transport almost halfway across the European continent to the ghetto in Riga, Latvia, rather than one of the death camps. At that time, they had no idea as to why this was the better alternative to where other transports were bound with their human cargo.

With ruthless efficiency and total disregard for hygiene, much less comfort, each of the cars was filled to capacity. Somewhere between eighty and one hundred people were literally crammed into the car. Clipboards were annotated, records transmitted to central archives, and with record efficiency, an undeniable history was maintained of these crimes against humanity. As these cars were being loaded, there typically were no steps to be utilized, and women, wearing dresses, holding babies, and assisting children, have to climb up into the car as modestly as possible. Once in the car, they stood pressed up against one another. Packed in with them was all that they were allowed to bring in the form of worldly possessions. These various and sundry bags, boxes, and pieces of luggage were usually all crammed into the same living space. The exception to this rule was when this transport was marked for immediate extermination, in which case, it was more expedient to have these items in a separate car. With barely any room to move around, all one could do was shift his weight from foot to foot.

In the summer, those in the cars battled the suffocating heat; as unwashed bodies press up against one another, and modesty had long since become a casualty. Summer sweat and filth were soon forgotten. In the winter, the wind blew the harsh cold in between the slats of the outer wooden walls, freezing those who were unfortunate enough to be against the walls of the car.

Unlike the metro in modern day Rome, or the subways of New York City, or the elevated trains of Chicago, there were no seats. What might be temporary discomfort measured in minutes for those passengers, would stretch into days and days for the inhabitants of the cattle cars. The cars bounced along the rails, sometimes requiring hundreds and hundreds of miles to pass beneath the heaving floors of the cars before the journey would be complete for those unfortunate enough to have been deemed enemies of the State. The deaths usually began on the second day.

As the ride continued, there would be stops for the crew to dismount and to take on coal or wood or water. There was time for the crew to stretch their legs, and to spell one another in the engine. For them there would be time to eat, to sleep, and to relieve themselves, all in a civilized manner. But for the human cargo, there was only an occasional opportunity for water, but certainly not food, and no time to stretch or to take care of bodily functions. At some of the stops, some of the dead may be removed, but the doors only open for an instant. They were quickly closed again; the heavy metal locks a signal reminder that they would remain closed until arrival at their final destination.

There was little air, and of course, sleep came in snatches, leaving everyone feeling as if they were walking zombies. It was not until the dead started to drop, later stacked like cord wood, that there was any room to move around whatsoever.

Upon arrival at the final destination, days and days after being sealed into what will become a place of death for at least a quarter of those confined, the doors opened, and the survivors were met by uniformed guards and dogs, who quickly ordered them to dismount to the train station platform, and to take all of their possessions with them.

As they dismounted, seemingly before they could even draw a breath of fresh air, they often were sorted to the left or to the right. One way meant continued life filled with back-breaking labor, for weeks or months; the other, almost certain instant death. Some were trucked, others marched, usually to the 'delousing' station where they would be met by other guards, who informed them that they stank and needed showers; and that their soiled clothing needed to be deloused as well. They were directed to remember where they left their suitcases and belongings, the deception maintained until the very end.

The humiliation continued when men, women, and children were forced to strip themselves naked in front of one another, modesty another casualty of this monstrous attack on mankind, as these unfortunate souls soon went to their deaths in chambers with false showerheads, the victims of the gas, Zyklon B.

For another group of living dead, their task was to clean up the cattle cars, to remove the corpses of those who could not tolerate the rigors of the journey, and to clean the cars to ready them for their next journey full of human cattle. In the corners and along the edges lay the remains of infants and old people, for they were the ones who usually could not survive this hell on rails. Their broken and trampled bodies were thrown from the trains like so much human refuse. Those doing this work dragged and carted away this additional fodder for the crematoria. All the while, the mounds of suitcases, clothing, shoes, eyeglasses, money, jewelry, and remaining food stuffs grow in ghastly piles.

We left Haltern on 20 January 1942, and were told to include with our belongings, enough food for a few days. We were transported by passenger train to Gelsenkirchen, which was the gathering point for the transport that would take us further. Those from the greater Recklinghausen and Dortmund district were told that Jews were being gathered for relocation in order that they would be able to work. With this as our only explanation, we had no firm idea that our destination was ultimately Riga, Latvia. We were in Gelsenkirchen for approximately two days, living in the giant municipal arena, which reminds me now of Madison Square Garden, merely waiting. We slept on the floor, subsisting on the food that we had brought with us from Haltern. I remember that there used to be all sorts of special events at the arena to include circus performers. For this reason, there were these great iron bars strewn all over the floor of the arena, and somehow while I was there, I took a terrible fall and in all likelihood dislocated my left shoulder. It pained me a great deal and did so for many years after liberation, until one day it just stopped hurting. There was of course no medical treatment available, so I just had to tough it out. My parents told me to tell no one about the injury for fear that it might be held against me.

It came time for our turn to be loaded into the cattle cars, and I remember being pressed up against my mother and my father, as they attempted to shield me from those around me with their own bodies. People were generally very docile, having already recognized that we were no longer free and that we had no choice but to follow the directions as they were given to us. We attempted to load all the suitcases in one spot just to have some organization within the car and to have some space to move. Unfortunately, people needed access to their bags because that is where they had food and other things that they needed to survive. Fights would break out because people were hungry, tired, and obviously very scared. Younger children crying for their parents, older people moaning about their own state; all so crazy and painful to observe.

I was fortunate enough to actually have had the best spot in the car because I was located right next to the bucket that had been provided for people in which to relieve themselves. Nobody else wanted the spot. I could sit in the corner, stretch my legs, and doze by leaning against the wall, but for the most part, we stood. The worst thing to deal with was the cold that seemed to creep into our bones. It made sleep hard to come by, and add to that, my shoulder was giving me a great deal of pain, and there was nothing anyone could do for me. I also remember how hard it was to move around.

There was a crude piece of wood across the top of the bucket. In addition to simply sitting on it, which got me off the ground, wrapped in my blanket, I was also later able to use it to stand on. Once I did, I could reach out between the strands of barbed wire that filled in the slats of the window built into the wall of the car. By doing this, I was able to break off icicles or bits of snow from the outside and pass them around so that we could have some moisture to press against our swollen and cracking lips -- it was a logical thing to do in order to promote survival.

Now, many people who I have told about this have visualized how badly it must have smelled to be near this bucket. What I soon learned is that there is a smell peculiar to death itself, and this stench was far worse than anything in the bucket. For when the spirit leaves the body and all that is remaining is the human shell, everything that was inside soon works itself out, and this smell is worse than anything else I have ever encountered.

I remember when people started to die. They would cease to make noise, and then they would simply stop moving. Or their husband or wife would start to cry out "Oh God," when their loved one died. It was very scary, especially for someone my age. Unfortunately, when people die, they still take up much needed space. As the days melted into one another, some of the people just started giving up, especially on the second and third days, and despite the smell coming off the corpses, others would lie down on them or at the very least use them as a pillow. We did try to stack them up off to one side in order to make room to move around.

Perhaps the only thing worse than these physical smells was the smell of fear that permeated the car. It afflicted everyone, young and old.

Both of my parents were tremendously traumatized by the journey in the cattle car; it was survival in its most basic form. My mother hardly spoke and was totally destroyed emotionally. She was full of despair, and my father was already greatly subdued. While never a talker, he was almost as quiet as a stone. It was extremely disheartening to me to see this once very proud man reduced so tragically by the degradation that was being heaped on all of us. I know that he deeply regretted not having sent me away on the *Kindertransport,* or not emigrating as a family when we had the chance earlier before *Kristallnacht,* or even immediately thereafter. I think the time spent in the *Judenhaus* had also left him bitterly defeated. The manner in which he had been treated as a German veteran soldier back in those two days of November, 1938, I think weighed very heavily on him. Physically, neither of my parents even resembled the people I remember them being prior to *Kristallnacht.*

While conversation was generally minimal, things would get animated within the car whenever we stopped. People would start talking loudly, wondering where we were, whether it was our final destination, and what would be happening next. But when nothing would happen and the doors would not open, everyone would get silent. Once we got moving again, things would settle down even more. But, if there is anything that I remember most of all about the entire journey, it is the fighting and the screaming.

The screams of old people who could not deal with the fear, the unknown, or death of a loved one, and the babies who cried because they were hungry or dirty. It seemed like the screaming would never end.

Every other day the doors would be opened and a couple of guys would be chosen to go and get us water. Naturally we were all warned that if there was any monkey business or any one tried to escape that they, and we, would be shot. The guards were there with their rifles, and of course, the ever-present dogs. The dogs would have been used to hunt down anyone attempting to escape. I don't recall any incidents out of the ordinary, because for the most part, people were too tired and too discouraged to try anything. What I do remember is that water never tasted so good. We had long since finished the food that we had brought with us from Haltern, not being prepared for such a long journey. At this time, we were also allowed to empty the bucket and to remove the bodies of those who had died. Fortunately or unfortunately, there were only about four or five people who died in our cattle car.

Our travel from Haltern via Gelsenkirchen-Dortmund was an eight-day ordeal. The train took us from Gelsenkirchen-Dortmund to Berlin to Danzig and into Riga, Latvia. The doors were finally opened, and we were allowed to disembark, after what I think was a total of six days in the cattle cars. I have been told by others on the transport more mindful of the time that we arrived in Riga on 29 January 1942. I had already learned that when you are laboring to survive under those horrible circumstances, time becomes absolutely meaningless.

CHAPTER 8

A Little Story: The Riga Ghetto

"I Promise You With My Life."

By late December, 1941, and into early January, 1942, the leadership of the Gestapo determined it was time to make all the small towns and villages Judenrein (clean of Jews). Notices were sent out that demanded all Jews come to their local town halls where they were informed that they were to be resettled, ostensibly for purposes of obtaining work – not necessarily employment – and some were actually told that their destination was Riga, Latvia. To afford them the "luxury" of this relocation, they would be required to pay the sum of 50 Reichsmarks per person for the trip, and were permitted to take an additional 10 Reichsmarks with them for incidental expenses. They were further instructed to pack one suitcase per person, not exceeding forty pounds in weight, of clothing and a blanket. Craftsmen were directed to take any specialty tools that they may still have in their possession, and what was believed to be an ample supply of food for an extended trip.

So it was that in late 1941 and early 1942, over sixteen thousand German Jews, including Natan, Lotte, and Alex Lebenstein, were rounded up and ordered for transport to the Ghetto in Riga. Immediately prior to the

Lebensteins' arrival, just after the first of the year in 1942, the population of the Jewish Ghetto was at 30,000. This level had been attained earlier, but kept in check through a wave of regular executions. The transport that the Lebensteins arrived on had come from the Dortmund area and had drawn from the districts around it to include Recklinghausen, Herne and Gelsenkirchen. This was the second to last transport to reach the Riga Ghetto.

In addition to being the capital city of Latvia, Riga had a large Jewish population in the late nineteenth and early twentieth centuries, and until the end of World War I, had, like its sister states Estonia and Lithuania, been part of the Russian Czar's Empire. As previously noted anti-Semitism was very common in Eastern Europe and had only grown in intensity in the 1920s and 1930s.

The ghetto in Riga was also an Arbeitslager (or Slave labor camp), and also a place for labor selection for other venues. Selection was another term for sorting, meaning that those who were too old or too young would be sent into the forest near Riga, murdered, and put into large mass graves that they themselves had dug or that had been dug by other slave laborers or Russian prisoners. The others, like Alex, were out-sourced and assigned to other, smaller slave labor camps and factories throughout Latvia.

Having a skill, i.e. butcher, tailor, mechanic, was often reason enough to permit continued life for Jews, even though they were constantly treated as sub-human. Engineers, doctors, lawyers, and teachers were of no value to the German war effort. Musicians were often kept alive, especially in the death camps, in order to serenade those arriving from the transports to maintain the façade that this was merely a relocation, and not immediate extermination. But by the end, when the Final Solution had accelerated to near breakneck speed, nothing could save the Jews.

The complete and final degradation and dehumanization faced by many of the Jews in the Riga Ghetto was what lay in store for Natan Lebenstein. From February through April 1942, the once skilled and respected kosher master butcher was relegated to work in the slaughterhouse, treating and curing the hides of the animals that were slaughtered there. Working with salt every day soon caused the skin on his hands to crack. The long workday became filled with pain as the salty brine continued to soak into his cuts. Soon the pain poured into the night as the skilled hands became septic, and then infected with tetanus.

While Alex and his mother and their immediate friends attempted to treat Natan it became evident that some form of serious disease was ravaging the body of this once strong and powerful man. Restlessness, chronic fatigue, as well as blinding headaches soon began to impact his ability to work. Suddenly, the telltale signs of lockjaw became apparent. The muscles in and around his face, neck, and particularly his mouth, began to grow rigid. In order to deal with the excruciating pain, he would sit backwards on a wooden chair and force his teeth deeply into the wooden back. Despite the lack of adequate heating supplies in the ghetto housing, he would sit there sweating, gnawing on the wooden chair, dealing with the pain. Without adequate medicines or treatment, this was the fate of young Alex's father.

On a cold, snowy January 29, 1942, the train stopped in what looked to me like No-Man's Land, a short distance from the station called Skirotava. We were told that those who were unable to walk the remaining four kilometer distance to the ghetto should stay with the cattle car, and that a truck would be along later to collect them. We had already figured out by this time that there would be no truck, and that anyone who was not fit enough to walk was only fit to die. There were some who did stay with the cattle cars, and they never did make it to the ghetto. They were taken to either the Rumbula or Bikerneki Forest for immediate execution.

The ghetto in Riga was initially for the Latvian Jews, who had all been ordered there. Some 33,000 of them were packed into this tiny isolated neighborhood. Originally they had kept to themselves in order to observe the Sabbath. Late in October 1941, the Germans, along with Latvian SS, took ten thousand Jews into the forest and shot them in order to make room for new arrivals. They started with the very young, the very old, the sick, and then the "less productive." On November 27-28, it was another 15,000 Jews, young and old, that were taken into the forest and brutally murdered. They then pushed the remaining Latvian Jews into different sections within the ghetto. One was for male Latvian Jews, another for female Latvian Jews. Once this was accomplished, fully one-third of the ghetto was now empty and ready to receive Jews from Germany, Austria, and other European countries. The streets of the ghetto were named after the various transports and the cities in Germany from which the transports originated. For example, there was *Dusseldorfer Strasse, Leipziger Strasse, and Koelner Strasse.* The street name also determined where the transports were unloaded and the people settled. We were part of the *Dortmunder* Transport and had our own little part of the ghetto in which we lived once we arrived there. The ghetto was a complete city unto itself with its own police station, hospital, and cemetery.

My father was called up to work in the slaughterhouse within the city. He could have been teaching them all the finer points of the meat industry back then, but instead he was assigned to salting and curing hides for leather. In normal times, it was one of the more degrading jobs in the slaughterhouse. It was very unbecoming to have a master butcher doing that. It should never have been. Sometimes there would be scraps of fat and meat left in the skins, and he would take his little knife and carve out pieces of meat that he would bring home with him at night. This would be added to the soup or whatever my mother could create from the meager rations we were given. As a result, during the 2 ½ months that he could work, we sometimes had a nourishing meal.

In April, he developed cuts on his hands from constantly having them exposed to and immersed in the salt used to cure the hides. The salt literally ate its way into the cuts. With no medication, it developed into blood poisoning, which in turn resulted in lock jaw. I will never forget it. It remains part of my worst nightmares. He would sit backwards on these old fashioned wooden chairs that had wooden slats on the back, shaking, biting into the top parts of the wood. His teeth left marks deep in the wood, and I can still see them as if it just happened. All my mother and I could do to help him and attempt to control the shaking from the convulsions was to give him some warm water to drink, but he could not swallow. We also tried to bathe his hands, in the hope of being able to draw out the pus and to take away some of the sting, but he would cry out in pain. So much pain! We witnessed him suffer, and we were unable to help him. He resembled a wild man, with his eyes bulging out, foaming from his mouth, and the muscles in his face frozen in a horrible grimace. He looked so out of control that he made us and the others who lived in the loft fear that he might be mad enough to attack us. He would arch his back and wail and wail. It is an image that I will never ever forget. It will remain with me forever.

When my father could no longer go to work, some guards came. I don't remember whether they were German or Latvian. Sadly, he may have been reported by some of the people who were housed with us. I don't know for sure. He was dragged down from our fourth floor quarters. Unable to walk, they had grabbed him under his arms and dragged him. He was screaming as they went down the stairs. The screams were so animal-like that it was hard to believe that they were coming from the man I had known as my father for fourteen years. It might have been the anxiety or the pain, I don't know for sure. He may have died going down the stairs, or they may have killed him. My mother and I looked out the window, and I remember that there was still a lot of snow on the ground. They had these huge sleds waiting in the street. Because of the snow, you really needed these sleds for transport. As we looked out the window, we noticed that there was someone lying on a sled, completely covered. We could only assume that it was my father, and that he was already dead. March had been his 62nd birthday. And that is how I lost my father. Information later reached us that he did die and was taken to the ghetto cemetery near the *Bielefelder Strasse*.

Probably the worst part about losing him under these terrible conditions is that we were not able to honor him. We were unable to mourn him properly, unable to sit *Shiva* or to pray for his departed soul in accordance with the Jewish religion or do the other things that would have allowed us to demonstrate the degree to which we honored and loved him.

During the time my father worked with the hides, I was in my first slave labor assignment located outside the Riga Ghetto, *Kommando 21*. The selection was made from three different transports which included some combination of Dortmund, Vienna, and Berlin. Under guard, we were marched out of the ghetto each morning and returned every night. We were charged with breaking up bombed out buildings. That meant that we were cleaning mortar off of bricks and the metal I-beams so that they could be recycled in order to rebuild buildings. All of the factories that had originally produced these building materials had been converted to supply materials needed in the war effort. 1942 was one of the coldest winters on record. As a result, the thin striped clothing issued to us provided little protection from the elements. With little food and drink, it really was survival of the fittest. The work was hard, but there was no alternative other than death.

The fact that I was big for my age and passed for older probably saved my life. Had I looked my age or been scrawny, worn glasses, or limped, I probably would have been selected for extermination. Because I looked sixteen, the assumption was that I had probably been one or two years into my apprenticeship as a butcher under my father. Of course the irony here is that by the time I could have begun my apprenticeship, my father had long ago been forced out of business. I guess time had become fluid for everyone. The fact that my parents were so much older probably also lent credibility to my being older too. All I knew at that time was that I was expected to work long hours, and I did. In some ways, work made the time go by faster.

Conversation with the other men of *Kommando 21* was limited on my part, mainly because of the difference in our ages, which made it in very difficult for me to relate to their memories of the "good old days." Add to that the fact we were all exposed to the bitter cold while we worked, conversation was really wasted energy. I spent most of my time listening to the older workers, hoping to pick up tips for survival.

It was shortly after my father's death that I too faced a life and death situation. At this time I was still part of *Kommando 21*, seven men from each of the three transports. Our men were constantly wheeling and dealing for food with the Latvian people, using whatever they had to barter. At this point I was so intent on keeping my nose clean that I would not have dared to attempt to smuggle anything back in. I never had anything to trade and really lacked the know-how to effectively barter.

On one particular day, we were stopped and searched for the first time. I can only assume that someone had observed the wheeling and dealing and had reported our group to the authorities. As a result of the shakedown at the gate, most of the group was caught with some contraband, and so all twenty one of us were marched off to the jail on Tin Square in the ghetto. We were all in one large cell. We were kept there for several days. The cell had a window that looked out on the sidewalk, but we were actually below ground, and it was only because I was tall enough that when I looked out, I was looking at people passing by.

Rumors abounded that we would all be killed. Nearby on Tin Square, visible from the window of our cell, was a set of gallows large enough to hang three people at once. Here I was, barely fourteen and a half years old, and I was not at all certain that I was going to see the ripe old age of fifteen. Still reeling from the loss of my father and already feeling the effects of frostbite, hunger, and the uncertainty that haunted me, I consoled myself by thinking about the goodbyes that I would want to say if I were to be hanged.

One day I was looking out of the window when I spotted a tall good looking woman – one of "our people." She began *to kibbitz* (joke around) with the [*Wehrmacht*] guard who was standing about twelve feet away. She was teasing and taunting him. Already at this age, and even under these trying conditions, I already had an eye and appreciation for a beautiful woman. Every so often she would look over at me, especially when the guard was distracted.

After a few minutes with the guard, she started to walk towards the window from which I was staring at her.

"Are you Alex?" she asked.

"Yes," I said tentatively, feeling my throat get both tight and dry at the same time.

"You are the youngest one in the jail. Do you know that?" she asked me.

"Yes so what?" I said to her.

"Don't worry," she said, and after making an effort to bend down on her knees, she proceeded to kiss me on the nose. Almost as quickly as she did this, she began to cry. When she started to cry, the guard who was watching our exchange began to laugh. As she stormed away from the window past the guard, she kicked the guard's rifle out from under him. I didn't know what to make of this, especially since I had never had a girlfriend, and this woman was definitely several years older than I.

She came again the next day. "They will not hang you," she said. "I promise you with my life."

I had my doubts, but I certainly liked the sound of that. At the same time we had been hearing rumors from visiting relatives of the other men that instead of all of us being killed, they were only going to kill the three oldest and the three youngest. Things were still not looking real good for me. My mother never came to visit me. I guess it was just too painful for her to see me in jail.

Hours passed, and all I could do to while away the time was to look out the window. Work on the gallows had long been completed, and at this point I had no idea what to expect. Another rumor was that they were going to kill one man from each of the transports as an example to the rest of us. Ultimately we heard that we were going to be spared because they needed the labor, but I was still too scared to believe anything. More hours passed, and still nothing happened.

The day came when the gallows were actually put to use in front of the entire ghetto population. Finally, they hanged the three oldest members of the group, and the rest of us were told that we were to be released from jail. We were forced to witness the execution of the oldest member of each transport that had formed *Kommando 21*. After witnessing the executions, I was finally released from jail but was then kept inside the ghetto doing menial labor. Some of it included cleaning the streets and sorting old clothes that came from our murdered people.

I later learned that my benefactor was in fact an Erna Hirshenhauser, the *Kommandant's* girlfriend. Apparently she had the "power" to persuade the *Kommandant*. It may also have been because young, strong men were needed for labor that he agreed to spare the rest of us.

The *Kommandant,* the lead Nazi there, was a man named Kraus. He was a bit of a psycho, and demanded complete obedience from both us and his own goons. He would march through the ghetto wearing his tall highly polished black jack boots. At times he had his dog and a whip in his hand. He was feared and always spoke in a low voice. I didn't have any direct interactions with him while I was in the ghetto, but I am certainly grateful that Erna did.

Next to Erna, the thing that I am most grateful for as I look back on the entire Riga experience is that I still have all of my toes. While working with *Kommando 21,* I developed a terrible case of frostbite. My shoes and feet became wet and stayed wet for what seemed to be forever. Eventually, as the shoes started wearing out and disintegrating, I learned a major lesson. When working in icy, snowy conditions, if I would wrap my shoes in burlap, which was quite effective at providing insulation, I could keep my feet relatively dry and warm.

CHAPTER 9

The Peat Bogs of Hasenpoth

"Like double loaves of Wonder Bread"

Like many of the countries of Northern Europe, Latvia stretched its coal and wood supply with the use of peat with which to heat homes. In addition to heating homes, some industrial factories also used peat. In 1942 and 1943, thousands of Jews were outsourced from the Riga Ghetto and sent to surrounding labor camps to become slaves in the peat bogs of Hasenpoth and other locations. While assignments such as this were often the result of a penalty being imposed, for either a real or trumped up rule infraction, this disagreeable labor was necessary to meet the demands for fuel from the industries supplying the war effort.

Workers lived in primitive barracks, surrounded by barbed wire and guarded by Latvian SS. A slit trench was the latrine, and there were poor facilities for washing or for medical attention. The conditions of the bogs, i.e. the acidity as well as the swarms of insects and lice, gave rise to infection and disease that would then run rampant through the barracks. The food was inadequate for work under these conditions, yet these men and women were forced to labor on, or to suffer the wrath of the sadistic guards.

After I came out of jail and had spent only a short time with my mother, who by now was on a cleaning detail within the ghetto, I was selected from a line-up to be sent to another location where I would be stationed for an indefinite time. I kissed my mother goodbye, not realizing that this would be the last time I was ever to see her.

From April until roughly September, 1942, I was one of about five hundred selected out to go to work in a small satellite slave labor camp in Western Latvia named *Hasenpoth*, or *Aizspute* in Latvian. We were trucked there and found conditions to be primitive. My primary job while in this camp was to shovel out peat from some of the bogs there. These bogs were huge holes surrounded by meadows. We stood in water that would start out ankle or boot deep and would often get to be chest high. We extracted the mud with iron shovels about twenty inches long and ten inches wide, with curved sides to keep the mud on the shovel. We placed it onto a conveyor belt where it would then fall into large tin molds that would make it look like double-sized loaves of Wonder Bread. The shovels full of wet peat were heavy, and the work was cold, dirty, and exhausting. The women, and some men on occasion, would then run the heavy wet molds into the meadow where they would dump it out onto the ground and return the empty molds for the next load. The sun and summer heat would dry the mud and shrink the loaves to one-third the original size. Sometime later, these loaves were then ground in a machine to a consistency resembling peat moss. I sometimes was one of the slaves moving the peat. If you weren't running and insuring that the tins were back to the conveyor belt, you would be accused of being a slacker, and severely punished. Such an accusation could have dire consequences in terms of punishment. In the event that the motor that powered the conveyor belt was not working, we would have to crank the belt by hand, another equally exhausting job.

Without any special waterproof clothing, we wore whatever was given to us that day. Sometimes it might be our striped garments, and other times it might be used clothing that had belonged to someone who was murdered. We would simply wear whatever was available that day. It really didn't matter, because as soon as you started working, you were wet and filthy. You could only stand to work this hard for short periods of time, so they would vary our assignments. The owners of the peat bog naturally wanted to keep their slave labor alive, so sometimes

I would shovel, other times I would run the peat, and sometimes I might even catch a break and be allowed to stay in camp for part of the afternoon. Sometimes they would split the day into shifts, and so we might leave camp twice in the same day, especially on the longest of summer days. Either we were working or resting. It is not like there was anything else to occupy our time. After our liberation, we learned that the peat produced by some *kommmandos* was mixed with human ashes from nearby crematorium in order to make the peat an even richer fertilizer or fuel.

Our typical day would start with a roll call very early in the morning, usually at first light, and then we would get something resembling coffee made from wheat or barley, and maybe a slice of bread with pig lard spread. In the evening there might be a little soup, or another piece of bread or a small piece of meat. Overall, we probably did eat a little better than other camps, because I don't recall ever feeling weak, and let's face it, we were important to the Nazis as slave labor. The day would end when it either got dark, or when the guards that were responsible for us decided that they had had enough for the day. I can't remember whether we worked in the rain or not, but what would it have mattered? We were wet anyway.

I guess I would have to say that I was just always lucky. Even though I was young, I was strong. There were those in the group that cared about me, insuring that I would get a break now and then. It seemed that no matter where I went there was either someone, or that invisible angel on my shoulder, looking out for me. I guess in some small measure I was always looking for a surrogate parent to me and to protect me to some degree. Part of that may have been that I was always the youngest in the group, or maybe just because God had other plans for me.

As one can imagine, it was hard, dirty work. Even though we could clean up with a shower at the end of the day, the lice in the straw bedding and in the clothing that we would change into insured that we continued to live in filth.

While I was in the bogs, I developed my first case of typhus. It was a mild case in that my temperature never spiked too high, and the strain that hit me resulted more in skin rashes, dizziness, and mild diarrhea. If you were too sick to work you could report to the nurse on sick call, who would confirm that you needed to stay and rest in the camp. Most of us were too afraid of doing this for fear of going on sick call and never being seen or heard from again. Fortunately, I was able to shake it after a short period of time. If I had not, it would probably have meant instant death for me because I would have outlived my usefulness.

The days were pretty much all the same. There was really nothing to distinguish one from another. When you were resting, you could still feel the effects of the work on your muscles which would be sore, and your mind would be equally tired. As there was no communication with the ghetto, I spent many nights wondering about my mother and praying for her safety.

When I peel away the layers of memory, the things that come most readily to mind about *Hasenpoth*, besides shoveling that horrible dark mud out of the bogs, were the smells. While the air outside was fresh, the air inside the barracks was full of mold and mildew, not to mention the smell of the people. We were living in makeshift tiered bunk beds in very close quarters. There was also the stink of infection, which is a unique smell that I will never forget.

I also remember the manner in which guards would often abuse us for no reason at all and give one of us a gun butt to the ribs or to the head. I got hit many times, but I don't remember why. Today my doctor cannot believe the x-rays of my rib cage; several old fractures that confirm the blows that I endured there.

With the change of weather in the fall of 1942, our assignment in the bogs came to an end, and we returned to the Riga Ghetto. Naturally I was looking forward to a reunion with my mother. Truly a Mama's boy, I was still full of hope. Looking back, I know it was the thought of seeing my mother again that had gotten me through the time at *Hasenpoth* and would continue to sustain me.

Upon my return I was told that my mother was no longer in the ghetto that she had been relocated and was on a transport to a new location. This was all that I knew until after the war. As a result, I did not know whether I should mourn or continue to harbor hope of seeing her again when the war ended. Ultimately, the truth is that she had outlived her usefulness. Having grown frail and not being overly strong or skilled, I now am certain that she was murdered in the forest outside of Riga, much like the thousands of others who were taken under the trees to be shot and buried in a mass grave.

Of course, not having the value of hindsight available to me back then, I was forced to believe that my mother had been transported out of the ghetto and was living elsewhere. I was probably fooling myself, but I clung to this hope as a means of survival.

Once I was back in the ghetto after my ordeal in the peat bogs, I was put to work again sorting used clothing and other menial tasks. In one of the nearby factories, I remember that we were put to work moving huge bails or rolls of material onto large cutting tables, while others, using patterns, cut out uniforms to be sewn for German soldiers to wear. It was these types of activities that kept me busy until late summer of 1943, when I was transported to the concentration camp, *Kaiserwald*, not very far from Riga. The ghetto was totally liquidated that following November.

CHAPTER 10

Potato Peels and Fishheads: Kaiserwald

"Not to diminish what he did, but there were lots of Oskar Schindlers … it was very profitable."

After the uprising in the Warsaw ghetto, in April, 1943, Heinrich Himmler, Hitler's architect for the Final Solution, ordered all ghettos in the Eastern portion of the Reich to be liquidated, and all Jews in the ghettos to be shipped to concentration camps. As a result of this decree, the Riga Ghetto was emptied, and its residents transported largely to Kaiserwald or one of the myriad of smaller satellite camps of which it was the hub.

Though it has many names, Mezapark in Latvian, Emperor Forest in English, it is best known by its German name, Kaiserwald. Located some seven miles from the city of Riga proper, prior to the war, it was one of the finest sections of forest in the region. It was where the wealthy of Latvia, regardless of religion or political affiliation, built spacious homes and estates that would, subsequent to occupation by the Russians, be occupied by the German invaders.

In late 1942, the camp was formed around a core of five hundred prisoners considered to be hardened criminals sent from Sachsenhausen.

Sachsenhausen was one of the older, original concentration camps established in 1933 by Hitler's henchmen. It was located on the outskirts of Berlin, and prisoners also included foreign born prisoners.

Alex Lebenstein joined the other inmates at Kaiserwald, and was there for a little over one year. He worked in a variety of capacities, most notably providing assistance in factories or performing menial tasks, such as peeling potatoes in the camp kitchen. Because of the increasing military drain on manpower, most of Germany's large industries had made a pact with Hitler and the Nazis, and were using slave labor as a means of meeting production quotas. The irony is that the factory owners usually paid a nominal daily rate to the camp commandant for the use of this slave labor in their factories.

In the absence of a crematorium, the Kaiserwald camp specialized in murdering Jews by means of gas vans. Those unfortunate enough to be condemned to death would be killed in these vans while en route to mass graves where they would be unloaded by other Jews. These work parties would often encounter a friend or even a family they knew. When this happened, and it became obvious, by means of lessening work effort, the effected worker might, in an instant, be the recipient of a bullet and join his family member or friend in the mass grave.

During the morning lineups, the trucks were gathered and people and work *kommandos* were assigned to the trucks. One never knew whether he was destined to be sent to a work site or to his death. Numbers would be called out, and each would board a truck, sometimes to simply disappear. We were long past the point of worrying or panicking. Let's face it, one way or the other, there was not a whole lot you could do about it. I just always assumed that I was going to my next assignment. I was young, healthy, relatively strong, and I kept my nose clean. I figured so long as I complied with orders and blended in I would not have to worry about being killed. With the war already going poorly for Hitler, labor shortages existed everywhere. Not to diminish what he did, but there were lots of Oskar Schindlers … it was both necessary and very profitable to utilize slave labor.

Near *Kaiserwald,* I lived in a huge abandoned clothing factory that contained large loom rooms. It was the only time that I was in a place where the men and women were kept in the same building, but in different areas.

The work detail that kept me busy the most was probably peeling potatoes. We subsisted on potato peels and fish heads. Fish heads have some good sweet meat on them, and when you cook them in water with potato peels, which have lots of vitamins, you can actually subsist on this soup. There were all sorts of menial work projects to be done. One day we went out and moved stones. Another day there was work in a factory. They kept us busy.

While in *Kaiserwald* we heard about mass graves all around us in Latvia. There were so many mass graves. Aside from illness, everyone who was killed there died with a bullet or in one of the gassing trucks and, in the absence of crematoria, was then buried in a mass grave.

I remember two brothers and a sister, all professional singers, who were inside the building hiding when the sub-camp was being liquidated. At lineup time, the guards, with the dogs, entered the building to look for them. They were shouting for them to come out, making promises that no harm would come to them. Well, we all knew what was going to happen if they came out on their own or were found. The dogs sniffed them out, found the two brothers, and rousted them out to the fire escape where they were immediately shot down.

I was in *Kaiserwald* until the fall of 1944, when they put us on a barge. Some of us thought we were going to be drowned. I was surprised when we were sailed out to a ship. I was on the ship for a while, and we were sailed down along the Baltic Coast to Hamburg, Germany. We were not needed there, and we were then sent back to the port of Danzig, Germany (Gdansk, Poland today). Some reports indicate only a two day cruise time, but I know, based on the stink and the filth of the ship that we were on it for many days more than that.

While we were on the ship, not knowing what would happen to us, we would often fall victim to our imaginations. All we could do was wonder what new form of hell on earth we would be exposed to next. Little did we know that we were being taken to a concentration camp, built on a smaller scale than the other more notorious death camps, but still worse than any place I had been before: *Stutthof.*

As I attempt to reflect back on this time, I realize that God has been good to me. I have blocked out many of the pain-filled times due to the anger and blind rage that consumed me for many years.

When life is cheapened as it was by the Nazis, the commodities of everyday life such as food, water, clothing, medicine, and heat take on a value greater than gold. Thoughts of a future did not exist; the day-to-day goal was to avoid trouble and to survive. This would be the largest challenge as we entered those gates of Hell known as *Stutthof.*

CHAPTER 11

Stutthof

"This is my last day."

Located about twenty miles east of the city port of Danzig, Stutthof became the first camp established in what had formerly been Polish territory, or East Prussia. Opened immediately after the Blitzkrieg of September 1, 1939, that formally began World War II, it was from its inception, designed to be a harsh labor camp and to hold "civilian prisoners of war," which meant anyone who was in opposition to the Nazi regime. It was soon populated with Jews and other "non-desirables" as well.

In 1942, due to growing demand, Stutthof was transformed into a concentration camp and was the center hub of a series of over seventy sub-camps to include the slave labor camp, Burggraben.

In the face of advancing Soviet forces on the Eastern Front, Jews from the three Baltic states of Latvia, Lithuania, and Estonia were sent to Stutthof in 1944. Most of those sent to Stutthof were women and children. The vast majority of those did not survive and contributed to the over 65,000 souls who lost their lives behind the wire there. Aside from those who were put to immediate death in the gas chambers or burned alive in outdoor crematoria, others died from the grueling conditions, hard labor, starvation and malnutrition, as well as disease, which was rampant in the camp.

By mid-1944, the gassing of Jews with the pesticide Zyklon B was the method of choice for a more efficient murder of thousands within the fences of Stutthof. The bodies were then burned in the outdoor ovens. This has been taken as evidence that the Nazis were so intent on intensifying the pace of their murderous business that they did not even take the time to enclose the ovens within a building.

While Stutthof was only one-tenth the size of some of the other better known camps such as Auschwitz and Dachau, it was still very much the same ruthless factory of death. With its chimneys towering over the camp belching human smoke thick enough to darken the skies around it, causing a hazy pall to remain nearly permanently in place, it was just as severe and just as deadly as the camps to the south and east.

With the Russians steadily advancing in the Baltic States and the Germans not wishing to lose any of their slave labor or allow any Jews to be liberated by Allied forces, the decision was made to close Kaiserwald, and all surrounding satellite camps. The first major exodus of Jews from Kaiserwald occurred in August, 1944. Approximately two thousand Jews were loaded aboard the ship Bremerhaven and sailed deeper into German controlled territory. In addition to being extremely overloaded, there was no food or water provided to the human cargo, and conditions were primitive. Once off the coast, barges were used to transport them to Stutthof where selection once again occurred. Men and women were separated, and then the old and the young were taken out. Those that survived selection were then faced with the horrors of surviving daily life in Stuffhof. Twice daily roll calls, facing the chimneys that continuously filled the sky with dark smoke, were often punctuated by the screams of those who could no longer withstand the rigors and the abuse, and would commit suicide by jumping on the electrified fence. If one was sick and reported this at roll call, that person simply disappeared into smoke.

We had heard that there were death camps in which there were gas chambers and giant crematoria, but I had never seen it until our arrival in *Stutthof*. It was a very sobering experience and death became a strong reality. I think a good number of people simply stopped caring. I was still harboring a small hope that my mother was alive somewhere and we would be reunited some day. The chimneys loomed very large when we arrived, and definitely were frightening to us. The smoke got in your clothing, in your hair, in your eyes, and even in your mouth. It was a horrible smell, and depending on the winds, would often leave a gritty feeling on your teeth. On rainy days, the smoke would fall to the ground like dirty snowflakes.

My first assignment in *Stutthof* was feeding mink, and then for a while assisting in the killing and skinning the mink for their pelts as well as the meat. Rather than opening the skin at the belly, it was pulled off whole, in one piece. The skins were then pulled inside out and stretched on a wooden board to dry them out. The pelts were used for military boots and uniforms, and of course, the brass used some of the nicer pelts to provide gifts for their girlfriends.

The meat was often fed back to the other mink, and on occasion some of us would eat some of it. While the smell attached to the meat was very strong, when you are hungry, you can eat just about anything. Naturally without any means with which to cook meat, we were eating it unwashed and raw. It was one means by which to garner some nourishment. I even remember eating dog once, and it was awful. It may be a delicacy in the Far East, but this was terrible. Of course it might have had something to do with the fact that the carcass had just been lying there and had not been slaughtered in a proper fashion.

One day I was told to collect the eggs from the hen house and bring them over to the kitchen located in the headquarters building. This was considered a real honor assignment. Sometimes I had enough courage to poke a hole in one of the egg shells and suck out the egg for nourishment. I would then crush and hide the empty shell in the hen house under the manure. I knew better than to leave any evidence of misdeeds lying around.

One could usually expect to spend quite a bit of time on the potato peeling detail. We actually peeled potatoes which would then be sent to the troops. We were free to consume the peels and would, on occasion, supplement our skins with some potato. We also were careful to make the rotten potatoes very evident among the peels so that the guards would not think that we were trying to steal potatoes.

When you were sorted, you never knew if it was your last day, or whether it was for a new assignment either in the camp or outside in another place. You were completely at the mercy of those who were poking and prodding you or allowing the dogs to nip at your heels. You finally reach a point where you are not afraid any more. They would ordinarily call us out by the number that we wore on our shirt and hat. By being a number rather than a person with a name, we were both degraded and dehumanized. It probably made it far easier psychologically on the butchers who were administering death if they could think of us as numbers rather than as human beings and pretend that they merely worked in a manufacturing plant.

One day, after the morning roll call, and following the day that I had done my little magic trick and sucked an egg out of the shell, I was sorted out of line. I was relatively certain that someone must have seen me do it and had turned me in. It was at this moment, while facing the chimneys of the crematoria belching out clouds of smoke, that I began to tremble, and I had the conscious thought that this was surely going to be my last day on earth. But almost as quickly as this feeling of fear appeared, it was gone, and I was resigned to my fate. Surely this was to be my last day. Imagine my surprise when, rather than being walked to certain death, I was walked out of camp to an awaiting train with real wooden benches. We were loaded aboard as if we were real passengers. Traveling like this, I felt reasonably confident that we were going to a place that would allow me to live a little longer. It was aboard this train that I was taken to a satellite camp near Danzig by the name of *Burggraben*, leaving the crematoria and death of *Stutthof* after only a short time which had felt like a lifetime.

I saw so much death. There are still sights and sounds that will often trigger memories and cause me to temporarily flashback to those times. Sometimes it will influence that night's dreams, but largely I live for today. I live for my children, my grandchildren, my great-grand children, my friends, and my work with the children. When I say prayers each morning, I don't pray for God to give me anything; they are simply prayers of thanks for all that I do enjoy now at this stage of my life.

I saw women, children, babies, old people, and young people, people deemed too skinny, too fat, or too near-sighted, separated out, and chosen for immediate death. I saw men beaten with rifle butts until they were dead. I myself was beaten in this manner on several occasions. Beatings from the guards, the *capos* (selected inmates used as ghetto police), and fights over scraps of food between inmates were so commonplace that one simply did not notice it after a while.

I saw people hanged, and left hanging as a lesson to the rest of us. Not to look at the body as it swung by its neck was grounds for punishment. There was a time that I was forced to contemplate my own death by hanging. I remember them building the three rope gallows out in front of my jail window.

Someone being shot was an everyday occurrence and something to which one soon became immune. It was something seen by young and old alike on a very regular basis. Over time, one even becomes emotionally numb to all of the brutality. I have bullet scars to remind me of the times that I was shot, but cannot remember when and where it happened. I also have scars from shrapnel that burned and sliced its way into my body that I do remember and will share with you later at the appropriate time in the story. Why I survived is anyone's guess.

I remember standing for hours and hours in roll calls two and three times a day, facing the chimneys of the crematoria belching out black clouds night and day, filling the sky with the horrible smell of burning flesh. If it was raining, the smoke would not rise in the air, and we would have grit and ash on our clothes and skin. Worse was the smell from the crematoria that permeated everything in the camp.

I have other memories that will linger forever. Some include the smell of death that accompanies bodies as they leave this earth. My first experience with that was in the cattle car ride from Gelsenkirchen to Riga. I next observed it up close while my mother and I treated my father in the Ghetto. I was exposed to it on a near daily basis while treating some of my friends in the various camps who suffered from typhus, lice, infection, and rotting flesh. A complete lack of sanitation gives rise to a whole new set of smells and odors that can turn the stomach at first, but becomes the norm over time. They all become part of daily life.

Death was everywhere, and yet there were those of us who continued to live, day by day, with no great thoughts of tomorrow. It was nearly impossible to think about anything other than simply getting through the day we were in. Survival was the only focal point.

The words that describe our daily existence are few, and can be covered with exhaustion, hunger, fatigue, thirst, lice, bitter cold, stench, mold, and, until the emotional numbness and surrender overwhelmed you, fear. You see, everyone reaches a point where they no longer fear the next roll call and separation, for we are already the walking dead. To live another day is a mixed blessing. It is another day of life, but it is another day in the hell on earth that was this life.

CHAPTER 12

Burggraben

"Melting From the Inside Out"

As the war continued, more and more men were being conscripted for service in the German Army. Older men and boys, previously not qualified, were now being issued uniforms and weapons. Because of this, the labor shortage afflicting German industry continued to become more and more acute. Once again, eyes turned toward the concentration camps and the nearly limitless supply of slave labor. Another selection in the concentration camp Stutthof formed a new kommando of Jews and non-Jews that was sent to a satellite camp in Danzig, known as Burggraben. Burggraben, meaning castle tower with a moat, was like other satellite camps in that it did not have a crematorium. Its main purpose was to supply forced labor. Conditions were primitive within the barracks. However, hygiene facilities and water were available to the prisoners. There was even a barracks just for the sick people. Food remained scarce, and the work on German U-boats being refurbished was long and arduous. Unfortunately, with no clean clothing to change into after a shower, everyone was soon infested with lice.

In January 1945, an epidemic of typhus broke out, and like a scourge, brought sickness or death to over fifty percent of those within the camp. The death count went so high that the Germans were forced to quarantine the camp for fear of having the epidemic continue to spread. With no medical treatment and the inability to keep food in their systems, more and more died.

In February, 1945, the Germans were once again looking to close the out-lying camps and to fall back deeper into Germany. When they attempted to evacuate the camp by marching the prisoners out, there were few who had not been afflicted to some degree by the typhus. Those who could muster the strength to walk were taken on what in most cases turned into a "death march." The vast majority of those who had been afflicted with the disease had already died. The others were simply too weak to move under their own power, and were left behind to die. Rather than wasting bullets and manpower, the Germans simply left, hoping that nature would take its course and that all would be dead prior to the arrival of the liberating Russians. Even after the Russians arrived on site, many more died due to the ravages of malnutrition or from the typhus.

Conditions in *Burggraben* were better because we were actually working in the Danzig shipyards refurbishing German U-boats. Being thin, my primary job was to paint the torpedo tubes with gray lead paint. My eyes would burn, and I could not breathe because the fumes of the paint were so strong. I had small brushes which I used to paint between the cables and wires that ran everywhere. I even had a piece of wood that I used to make a template to enable me to paint behind the wires. It was important to do a good job because if your work was inspected and it did not look up to standard, the punishment and consequences could be severe.

The saving grace to this type of work is that we went long stretches without supervision, which in turn allowed us to rest and to take a breather. I was especially grateful for this when I was so sick. There was no alternative but to work, but at least I could stop and rest and gather my strength. When I would hear footsteps approaching, I would naturally go back to full work status.

The food was a little bit better because of the nature of our work, so it might mean an extra portion of soup, or an extra slice of bread, or an extra meal in the evening when we returned to the camp. At this point, we were very important to the war effort, whether we, or the Nazis, wanted to admit it.

They wanted us clean to work on the submarines, so we were encouraged to shower. But with only dirty clothes to get back into, the shower served little purpose. We were all full of lice. The lice were in every crack and crevice on our bodies, in the beds, in our clothes, under our scabs, they were truly everywhere.

One day, shortly before our liberation, I found myself in the position of performing "surgery" in *Burggraben*. A friend of mine developed a severe case of typhus and had one huge bed sore on his buttock, and I lanced it for him. I found an old rusty scissor and sterilized it in a pot of boiling water. I made a slit in the boil and there was hardly any reaction from my friend because the infection was already deep and causing him great pain and high fever. He was hardly aware of what I did. But almost as quickly as I lanced the sore and removed the infection and lice, his fever broke and he began to recover.

In the coming days, when the Russians were advancing, we had an unwanted ringside seat to the battle between them and the Nazis. We could hear artillery fire, tanks battling, and hear and feel the aircraft in the sky overhead. We would stay inside the barracks and hope that it would provide enough shelter to help us avoid being killed.

My friend had gained enough strength that he was soon able to climb to the top tier of our bunks, and I could stand there and we would have a conversation face to face. He was actually lying there on the bunk, propping himself up with one hand holding up his face, and me standing next to him. We were having a conversation, when all of a sudden I realized that he was not answering me. My first thought was that it would have been an odd way for him to have fallen asleep, especially propping himself up the way he was doing. Then blood suddenly started spouting from his mouth, drenching me. A bullet from a strafing [Russian] plane had come through the roof and hit him right in the chest. He was gone in a second. In an instant, we went from having a conversation to his being dead. It could have been me. Yet, for some reason, I was spared death again.

There are certain smells or "stinks" that will take me back to that time as if it were only yesterday. The smell that emanated from my father's hands as they were becoming infected and he was developing lockjaw, or the stink that came off the infected skin of people I was forced into contact with on a regular basis, will forever remain with me.

A day or so later, while I was walking in the camp, mortar fire resumed. I heard the explosions and dove under a nearby hay wagon. But before being completely shielded by it, hot shrapnel penetrated my buttocks. It burned terribly. Unlike bullets that often go through and through, this was hot and merely burned itself into my skin. When I tried to pull it out with my own fingers, I burned them. Some of it was removed with pliers by my friends in the barracks, and later, the deeper pieces were removed by the Russian doctors that accompanied the soldiers who liberated the camp.

I have a recollection of being marched out of the camp by older German soldiers. They were neither SS nor SA. They were simply old men who had been pressed into service. We were marched a distance from the camp. It was cold, but the ground was muddy. We were probably no more than an hour from the gates of the camp. They suddenly made us stop, sit down, and we were told to stay where we were. One by one, they all started disappearing into the woods, as if they were going to relieve themselves. The amazing thing is that they never came back. This was supposed to have been the start of a death march back to Germany, but all of a sudden we were on our own. The guards that had marched us out of the camp had disappeared.

Most of us were too sick and too weak to take any chances on trying to survive in the woods. We sat there weighing our options, and realized that our best bet was to return to the camp, so we turned around and followed our tracks back to *Burggraben*. It was very shortly after our return to the barracks that the air war over the camp became very intense, with bombs and mortars exploding all around us. It was so severe and so frightening that we finally left the barracks and took shelter inside something like a potato hole. What made it unique was that it was a permanent, hardened hole like a root cellar. It had two doors that covered it and had four or five concrete steps down into it. We sat there for over an hour, when all of a sudden it became quiet, deathly quiet. It was as if everything had stopped. We didn't know if we should stay there or get out. We didn't hear any shooting or shouting and wondered where the camp guards had disappeared to -- they had obviously abandoned us and the camp.

Suffering a second case of typhus, I could barely move. My fever was very high and I felt as if I were melting from the inside out, meaning that I could not keep a drop of liquid in me. Everything that I put into my mouth would find its way back out in one form or another. I probably would not have survived had liberation occurred even a few days later.

For many hours, or perhaps a day or two, we were completely on our own. The guards were gone, but there was still shooting from the air and isolated pockets of fighting going on. As a result we were back and forth to the root cellar several times. Some foraged in the kitchen for whatever food they could find. Of course, I was so sick that I could keep nothing down, so it did not matter what I put into my mouth. I was so sick that I could only get around by crawling on the floor or by holding on to another person. At one point we re-entered the root cellar and simply stayed down there.

Every so often my older and very resourceful friend Zompka would go up the stairs and peer through the crack between the doors to see what was going on. I was very fortunate to have had a friend like Zompka at that point in my life. We preferred to converse in Yiddish because the German language was so distasteful to us.

Suddenly the doors were ripped open, and these Russian soldiers entered the pit, storming down the stairs, pointing their rifles, sweeping the entire pit, looking for German soldiers, ordering us in Russian to stay still, put our hands up, and not to move. Fortunately, Zompka spoke Russian and was able to greet them with "brother," and he identified all of us as Jews.

I was so sick that I have no sense of how long a time we were down there in the root cellar with the soldiers before a Russian officer came down the stairs wanting a report of what they had discovered. Zompka started speaking in Russian, and the Russian officer, identifying himself as a Jew, responded in Yiddish, inquiring as to whether we were Jews. When Zompka answered affirmatively in Yiddish, the Russian officer assured us that we were now out of danger.

While we were waiting for whatever assistance the officer had directed, he wanted us to tell him everything we could about where the Germans might have gone or where other Germans might be positioned or hiding. The Russians were aware that German troops remained in the area, within two kilometers of our camp, because the Germans had fired a great deal of flak in the air while the Russians were engaged in bombing and strafing the area. The problem they had is that they could not pinpoint where the Germans were. We were able to tell them exactly because these anti-aircraft sites were relatively permanent, and some of us had even helped to lay the concrete for them. When our groups went to put the concrete down, we always walked from camp, and so it was not uncommon to count your steps either out of boredom or as a means of having something to concentrate on. As a result, we were able to say "three thousand or five thousand feet, through that forest" to pinpoint these locations and the Russians were able to drop rounds directly on them.

Before we knew it, several covered trucks drove up, and we were loaded very gently into the back of them. We were then taken into the city of Danzig to a hospital that had been converted from an old schoolhouse, where our wounds were cleaned and our typhus treated. This involved the removal of all the scabs covering our wounds, shaving us of any remaining hair and cleaning our bodies from head to toe to rid us of the lice and lice eggs with which we were infested. Even without antibiotics, within a day or two, I was able to eat soft foods such as mashed potatoes, seasoned with a little onion or butter, or potato soup, and slowly I began to recover.

A few days later I was able to walk around, and with each passing day I became stronger, especially after I was able to eat the more varied diet that the Russians had to offer us. They would often cook everything in one giant pot, and we would refer to it as *eintopfgericht*, or "all in one pot." The Russian's black bread was very nutritious because it was all natural flour, unbleached, with whole grain, which also made it more substantial. I promised myself that I would never take food for granted again.

CHAPTER 13

Liberation

"The Most Important Job"

Thanks to the Russian liberators, their medical staff, and the proper food I received, my body soon mended. However, nothing they could provide to me would heal the emotional wounds that threatened to devour me. At the time that I was liberated by the Russians in March, 1945, I was both bitter and angry towards Germany. As I was physically recuperating, I had the time to reflect back on my lost childhood, the terrible suffering we all went through, the painful death of my father and the uncertainty associated with my mother's status, I found myself uncontrollably angry. There were times that my mind only thought in terms of revenge. As my mind wandered, it went to thoughts of killing any German adult, child or dog that I might encounter. I even went so far as to envision flying a plane and dropping a few bombs on the city of Haltern in order to kill as many as possible, if not the entire town, if it turned out that my mother had not survived. It never occurred to me that I would be killing many righteous people and past friends of my family. I was already coming to the realization that despite the defeat of the Nazis, my life was never going to be as it had been, but I remained resolved to going home to Haltern and finding my mother. For if through some divine act she had survived, I knew that I would find her waiting for me in Haltern.

Except for these severe feelings of anger I was still emotionally numb. My emotions had simply shut down long ago. After watching the beatings, the shootings, the hangings, and being constantly reminded that I could die at any moment and simply become part of the never ending black smoke going up the chimney of the crematoria, I was not feeling anything with the exception of raw anger. What made this dangerous is that it was unfocused. I was just angry at everyone and everything around me.

Life seemed distorted, deranged, and I remember being so sensitive to noise and movement around me. These sensitivities linger to this day. I think everyone was distrusting, even of friends, because at this point, it would be true to say that it was every man for himself. It was this attitude that gave rise to my wanting to first kill Nazis or every German, and then later the British, when I was training in the DP camp, ready to take my place as part of the *Hagganah* in what would shortly become the State of Israel. Perhaps most disturbing to me was the fact that this anger could even be turned toward my own people [fellow Jews] if I thought that they were trying to get the best of me.

People often ask me what I remember most about being liberated, and I tell them that my memory of it is clouded. Were it not for Zompka who reminded me later, I would not be able to describe the liberation in the detail that I do. I was so sick and so feverish, between the typhus, the mortar and bullet wounds, and the lice, that I was nearly completely debilitated and very weak. While I began to improve almost immediately after being deloused and having my wounds cleaned and treated, it was probably ten days before I really began to feel like myself. Of course, there was still a war going on around us. There was no safe place to go, as the entire area was full of soldiers, snipers, and bombs being dropped and exploding.

It was painfully clear to me that death was still all around me. Dead people and dead animals littered the countryside for as far as the eye could see. Bombed out buildings and bridges brought with them a feeling of utter sadness. So much waste, so much pain. In essence, there was no place to escape to safety. As a result I was willing to stay at the hospital in Danzig and to assist the Russians in the treatment of the other patients.

The Russian doctors were treating the other survivors in the same manner as they had treated me and facilitated my recovery. The cure for typhus was basically to get rid of all of the lice and vermin that were infesting our bodies. Whenever possible, we burned the clothing that the person had been wearing, replacing it with whatever was available and free of lice.

It was shortly after I agreed to assist in the treatment of my fellow survivors that I was directed to the kitchen by the Russian officer in charge, and according to him, given the "most important job" in the hospital which consisted of tending the fires under huge cauldrons of boiling water. I did this from April until June. What made this work so important is that this was the sole means by which they sterilized the surgical instruments, washed and reused the bandages, and treated the sick. A smaller pot of water was kept boiling for tea for the Russian officer/doctors whom I would serve whenever they yelled for tea. It was a constant state of noise and confusion as these doctors worked very hard to save many people who were suffering.

In the month of June, a couple of my newfound friends and I were presented with the opportunity to enlist in the Army and to serve Mother Russia. The Russian officer who attempted to recruit us said something like, "We liberated you; you owe us your lives, so now you can serve in our Army." Well, it did not take too much thought to realize that as foreign nationals enlisting in their army we would have been given the worst jobs, and probably would have been nothing more than cannon fodder had we joined. We avoided the officer for as long as possible as we tried to buy time before we were forced to sign up. We did everything imaginable to avoid this officer for many days.

After a week or so of our artful dodging, it was now early July, we were once again summoned to see the officer attempting to recruit us. The war was over, but he was still insistent on having us join the Russian Army. We were really in a tight spot now, and after my friend Zompka looked at the Russian enlistment papers a second time, he asked for just a little more time to translate the papers for our other buddy, Ewald Aul and me, so that we could all consider the generous offer. When that request was granted, we quickly left, and planned our departure. Recognizing that we were definitely out of time before the Russian officer would really press the issue, we decided that we needed to get while the getting was good. We grabbed what little we had and left that night.

We were actually fortunate enough to steal three horses from the hospital stable and to leave on horseback, determined to take our chances out in the forest. As we began our journey, we found and took better clothing, as well as uniforms, guns, and ammunition off the numerous dead bodies that we encountered along our way. After so many years, it was wonderful to be wearing good boots on my feet. It was even better to be rid of the rags that we had become accustomed to wearing, and to have real clothing to wear. We however took the uniforms along as an insurance policy.

Of course it was still very dangerous. There were snipers from both sides hiding in the forests, in abandoned farm houses and villages, because war does not just stop all at once just because the big shot brass says that the war is over. There are always pockets of resistance, so we had to be very careful as we made our way.

There was an occasional live farm animal that we would see, but for every one alive, there were dozens of dead ones. Their legs were stiff, their bodies bloated, or if their rotting bodies had already exploded, they were covered in flies and vermin. There was death to be seen all around us.

We abandoned our horses when we found cars and military vehicles in different states of repair and ruin. One might be better than another, or simply have more gasoline in the gas tank, so we would siphon it out and put it into whatever vehicle we were set on using.

Thus we made our way toward the town of Frankfurt am Oder. We had to wait and hide out on the Polish side of the border until the railroad bridge that crossed the River Oder was repaired. Our plan was to grab a train and cross over to Frankfurt am Oder and get to Berlin, and eventually into the American Zone of Occupation. From The American Zone we would be able to go to our respective home towns and determine what life had to offer us there. As we hid out and waited, I was left to daydream about all the different ways I could meet my mother and we would be reunited. I often found myself smiling at these thoughts, for at heart, I was still a Mama's boy. My thoughts would run to the things that we would say to one another, the food that we would eat, and the possibility of enjoying some of the simple pleasures that we had enjoyed before the Nazis had destroyed our lives, such as sitting on our gazebo on a beautiful summer night.

CHAPTER 14

There's an Alarm out for You

"I told them to take a swim"

The American Jewish Joint Distribution Committee (JDC) was the primary vehicle for relief operations conducted during and after the war by Jews in America. During the war it funded orphanages, hospitals, and public kitchens. The JDC also provided funds for food parcels and false papers and identities to be sent to Jews, even in ghettos and concentration camps.

In the four years immediately following the war, the JDC was able to raise and distribute nearly $300 million dollars in food, clothing, books, school supplies and other necessities. After the founding of Israel, the JDC helped transport refugees to Israel and established vocational training centers.

So it was that I, along with my friends Zompka and Ewald Aul, hid from the Russian military who we thought might be on our trail, until we could cross the river and catch the train that we hoped would take us all to the freedom of the West, and me, closer to home.

Finally, the workmen finished the bridge repair, and one day we heard the sweet whistle of an approaching train. As the train slowed, we were soon able to get on to it by running along side, and with some of the weapons that we had found in the forest, we took control of the engine. I am relatively certain that the engineer had only one thought on his mind and that was not to anger us for fear that we would kill him. As the younger "German" in the group, it was up to me to talk to the engineer and to instruct him to get the train moving and to keep it moving. At this point we were probably wearing some of the Russian uniforms we had acquired during our time in the forest. We also kept civilian clothing in the event that we might need them. All in all it was a very gutsy thing to do. Once the train was moving again, the engineer informed us of the presence of Russian soldiers in the caboose. Zompka made his way back to the caboose on top of the rail cars, where he found three Russian soldiers.

When he later came back to the engine I asked him, "Zompka, what did you do to the soldiers?"

"I took care of them," he said mysteriously.

"What do you mean that you took care of them?" I persisted.

"I told them to take a swim."

The manner in which he said this left no doubt that the subject was closed, so I stopped asking any additional questions. The rest of the trip on the train was uneventful.

We were fortunate that the German engineer from the train was very nice, and probably still a little scared of us. He told us that he was familiar with our past and wanted to help us out of sympathy for the manner in which we had suffered. He told us that he knew what had happened to us was very horrible, but he hastened to assure us that he had neither been a solider nor a Nazi. Rather, he had spent the entire war driving his trains, and moving people and equipment to where it was supposed to go. Could it have been our people or even my parents and me on one of his trains? While I did not ask these questions, they hung silently in the air. He helped us by telling us when to get off the train to avoid being detected. He then pointed us in the direction in which we should head in order to safely cross into the American Zone.

I was still without identification papers at this point, but I was far from alone in this predicament, for there were many people without papers. From the time we left the Russians to begin our journey West, we were constantly encountering people who were looking for someone that they had lost. There were the people from different camps looking for loved ones. The conversations were always pretty much the same. "Which camp were you in? Did you know someone called …? When was the last time you saw them alive? Do you know where they were going?" It was all so sad, because most of the time, the people they were looking for were dead; either shot or gassed, buried in a mass grave or shoveled into an oven. It would have been heartbreaking to tell these people the truth about their loved ones if we had known anything or if we could even feel anything. The numbness that we all had developed in order to survive without going insane more often than not kept us from feeling anything for these people.

Sometimes, however, there would be news of a person, and those who were doing the seeking would take off and wander to the city or town that their loved one had last been seen, only to be disappointed. It was very confusing, very frustrating, and very sad. I would learn of this bitter disappointment later myself.

In addition to these poor and often pathetic people, there were also many many homeless Germans who had literally been bombed out of their own homes by the countless Allied bombing raids that had taken place in an effort to beat the Nazis into submission. I would later learn that this number was in the hundreds of thousands, if not the millions. We were quite a collection. People were constantly moving. Quite often they did not know where they should move to or not move to. It was a very confusing time. The war was officially over, but there was also a lot of disagreement between the allies as to who would govern which parts of Germany and most notably Berlin. There was also a great deal of lawlessness. Murder, rape, and robbery – it was rampant. It was as if law and civilization had ceased to exist. It was as if we were all pawns on a giant chess board. All I knew for certain at this point is that I wanted to get back to my hometown of Haltern because if my mother was alive, that is where I would surely find her waiting for me.

We were in Berlin for over two weeks. Once we were in the American Zone we fell under the supervision of the Joint Distribution Committee

(JDC) and they fed us and insured that we had proper shelter. We were kept out of the public eye because the Russians were still looking for us according to a few of the people who first greeted us with looks of amazement and "You guys are alive? There's an alarm out for you."

Zompka wanted to go East to seek his family, so we parted company, and I never saw or heard from him again. Ewald elected to stay with me. By this point, I was more than a little restless and certainly anxious to continue my journey towards Haltern. I was convinced that I would find my mother waiting for me there, or all hell was going to break loose!

The Zones of Occupation were very confusing. Haltern was in the British Zone. Ewald and I had to cross back into the Russian Zone in order to get into the area controlled by the British so as to catch a regular train. As we left the greater Berlin area, we were able to get seats on a regular train. It was a traditional European railroad car with passenger compartments that contained benches that faced one another, with an overhead luggage rack.

While we were leaving a train station, a young lady was attempting to board the train in a hurry. She was shouting, "Please take me, please take me." The doors had already closed and were locked. I opened the window located on the door and offered her my hand and pulled the girl up through the window. I must have pulled harder and with more strength than was necessary, because she landed up in the luggage rack. She stayed up in the luggage rack either curled up, or sitting with her legs dangling over the edge. After several hours, she asked whether she could come down. I told her that she could, but with there being no open seats, she had to sit on my lap. All of us were sitting knee to knee, so it certainly was a tight fit. Even after what I had been through, as a man of nearly eighteen years of age, I found it a very pleasant experience to spend some time with an attractive young woman in this manner.

CHAPTER 15

Home to Haltern

"If my mother is going to be alive, she will meet me at the house."

No one who meets Alex today would ever consider that this is a man without a college degree, much less only a third grade education. His command of the English language is impressive and the articulate manner in which he expresses his thoughts and feelings is amazing. One can only believe that, but for the war and its ugly intrusion into his young life and the disruption of his education, Alex would surely have been a man of letters and accomplished even greater things than he has done in his life. Down to earth, he deals with the people around him with a commanding presence, but always from his heart and soul. This was not the case however when he returned home to Haltern after an absence of over four and one-half years.

By the end of August, 1945, Ewald and I finally arrived in Haltern. In my heart, I believed that if my mother was still alive, she would meet me at the house. What I really hoped to find was that my mother had returned before me and was already living in our home. Even as I approached my eighteenth birthday, I was still very much a Mama's boy. I wanted to find her so together we could reclaim our home and begin to rebuild our lives in Haltern. The hope of doing just this was the source of my courage and ability to go on even during the darkest of times over the past three and a half years.

With my heart pounding and trusty Ewald at my side, we approached *Disselhof Strasse.* I pictured my mother there to greet me, lovingly, with open arms. When we came to *Disselhof 36,* it was only to find that my home was no longer my home. My mother was not there. The neighbors told me that she had never returned. The people living in our house were not even the same people who had occupied it after *Kristallnacht.* It had changed hands several times in the interim. The current occupants had bought the house from another person who had bought it from someone else who had bought it after the bank had foreclosed on it when my father was no longer allowed to earn a living -- like all Jews who could no longer practice their professions due to the revocation of their licenses. I tried to be forceful with the people as they stood in the doorway, very loudly demanding our home, but they would not yield. But then, why should they give up their home to a stranger?

From there I went over to the city hall and attempted to get someone to help me understand why my house was no longer my house. This is another instance where my lack of education and knowledge really hurt me. It soon became very apparent to me that I was getting nowhere fast. So, to draw attention to my dilemma and to let them know that I was quite serious, I picked up a chair and threw it over the counter, and it splintered into pieces. Needless to say everyone who was in the city hall stopped and stared at me when the chair exploded as it did. I was then in the process of lifting a desk with every intention of upending it too, when two guys grabbed me. It was probably good that they did. What is amazing is that despite these outward shows of anger, I thought I was being both adult and reasonable. Did they not realize what I had gone through? Could they not feel my pain? Did they not realize why we had lost our home in the first place? At that point I still had every expectation that I would be living there among former neighbors. I was still operating under the assumption that I had come home. I didn't know from anything else. My goal at that point was to stay there and to pick up the pieces of my life.

Despite my outward acts of immaturity, the city elders prevailed upon the people who now owned my parents' home, and they made room for me to stay with them. They were told that while they were under no legal requirement to do so, that it would be nice if they could accommodate me while we were "sorting through" things. So I slept on an old sofa bed in what ironically had been my parents' bedroom for most of the time that I stayed in Haltern. I remember having the thought that the last night I had slept in that room had been November 9, 1938, which was the first night of *Kristallnacht*. I had slept with both of my parents. We had been a family and had passed that fateful day with no disruptions in our little town. Now I was alone. The emotions that I experienced ranged from sadness and despair to utter hopelessness and totally consuming anger. But then again, it appeared that many of the townspeople were having the same feelings toward life in general and me specifically. In my mind, the slogan that had been drilled into them by the Nazis, *Die Juden sind unser Ungluck* ("the Jews are our misfortune"), was haunting them at this time. I felt they now saw in me, the sole surviving Jew of Haltern, lashing out in his anger, the one who was indeed responsible for their own misfortune.

In reality the war was still going on. There was no shooting, but the hatred was very much still in evidence. It was clear to me that the Germans felt the defeat very keenly and what better place to let this anger and frustration out than on this "Jew bastard" who had the audacity to return. Never mind that Hitler led the country into ruins. I believed in their minds they were probably thinking: "It is because of this Jew bastard (me) that we are all now suffering. He is still alive and yet my father or grandfather died." I don't believe it ever occurred to them to give a single thought to my losses: the murder of my parents and members of my extended family. Did they realize I was the only one left? The anti-Semitism was as strong as ever. While I no longer walked in the gutter or wore the yellow Star of David on my clothing, I felt the hostile stares, and in some instance the seething anger, as I walked the streets of Haltern. I recalled my earlier mindset and the hopes that I had for receiving a true welcome back to Haltern. I had hoped that a welcome of this nature would alleviate my desire for vengeance on the people of this town. Instead, I had to fear for my life.

There were instances where it was plainly obvious that some people were afraid to talk to me, fearing that I remembered them and their participation in degrading us and destroying the lives and properties of Jews, or simply because they had heard of my angry outbursts. They were so afraid that they would often cross the street and avoid eye contact with me. It was this realization that brought on such frustration and conflict and gave rise to what I refer to as my "destructive anger period."

On one occasion while I was crossing into the marketplace, I ran into another of my former classmates with whom I had also played soccer. I greeted him with open arms and a broad smile on my face. I told him that I had only recently returned to town. He responded by telling me that he knew that I had been incarcerated, and that he himself had just returned from time as a prisoner of war in connection with his service in the Army. When I pursued this line of questioning and asked him exactly when he had gotten back, he responded that it had been about two months before. So I asked him how come he was still wearing his old uniform. He became visibly angry at the question and assuming a military posture, proclaimed that he was proud of the uniform. He then patted the upper sleeve of his *Wehrmacht* uniform jacket where the eagle and swastika was and proclaimed that he was proud to be a German soldier. Seeing him in that horrible uniform made me absolutely furious. When he told me that I was just a "damn Jew" and that I had no business being in Haltern any longer and that I should go away before he and some of his other friends would kill me, I literally saw red. So I said to him, "What are you doing? Why are you wearing that horrible uniform? The war is over!"

He then replied something to the effect that it was "all your (my) fault" and that he was proud of having served the Fatherland. Between the uniform, his attitude, and his inflammatory words, as well as my quick fuse and deep-seated, explosive anger, I started beating him. I ripped off his uniform jacket and tore it to shreds. As I did this, he cried out, "What are you doing? I love my uniform." Needless to say I beat the tar out of him until he ran off.

By the middle of October, it was very clear to me that my days in Haltern were definitely numbered. The attitude of some people, as well as the incidents and confrontations that I had already experienced, convinced me that I was surely not welcome. My impression was that there were many Nazis still living in the town who would gladly relish the opportunity of harming or even killing the sole surviving Jew of Haltern.

The knowledge that I had to leave my home town made me more and more bitter with each passing day. When added to the feelings that I already harbored with the realization that my mother had been murdered and was not going to be a part of my life as I had dreamed, my anger knew no bounds. I felt as if I were a ticking time bomb ready to go off at any moment. I guess one of the reasons that it took fifty years for me to even consider going back to Haltern was the circumstances under which I left it again in 1945.

People who had been friendly to my parents or to me as a child finally warned me that the town was not a safe place for me to be right now. Some of them cautioned me, "They are out to get you." They also convinced me of the futility of attempting to get my family home back. They pointed out that it had been mortgaged, that my father had defaulted on the loan when he failed to make payments, long before we went into the *Judenhaus*. Clearly, they never gave a thought to the repressive laws that had robbed my father and others like him of their licenses and the ability to carry on a business. They had somehow also forgotten how even in the early 1930's, the propaganda, "Do not purchase from Jews," had kept them away. I was told that the people living in the house now were the lawful owners of it. The property had actually changed hands several times, with each transaction being completely legal. They pointed out to me how naïve it was of me to think that by simply reappearing after seven years that these people would either voluntarily, or upon order of the City, simply pack up and leave the house that they had legally purchased, and allow it to revert back to me. I know that I did not want to hear that from them. My anger caused me to turn a deaf ear, and my rage was making me blind. A few of our former friendly neighbors actually said to me that I should go away for a while and then come back when things had more fully calmed down. They even gave me some cash. I know now that they were not telling me to stay away forever. These were good people. When I told them that my parents had been murdered, they practically tore their clothes in grief, just as an Orthodox Jew would have done in an effort to honor a loved one who had passed.

After these incidents and despite the good counsel from people who did care about me, I believed that I was no longer safe in Haltern and that greater harm could come to me, or I could really hurt someone, if I did not leave. I departed Haltern on a motorcycle that I cannot recall how I acquired, and went to see my friends Margie and her younger brother Joachim Hoffman in the city of Oelde.

For some reason, they had been able to reclaim the home of their parents. I found Margie ill and shivering with fever wrapped in a blanket. She was especially happy to see me, having just returned from the local hospital where she was refused treatment. They turned her away because she had no medical insurance and because they would not treat Jews. She asked me to take her to the family Spiegel, former friends of her parents, who had survived and were again living in nearby Warendorf. I took her there on my motorcycle. At the time of this writing, Margie is still alive and well, and resides in Skokie, Illinois.

Not knowing where I should go or live, I took Margie's advice to check out the DP camp in Deggendorf, Bavaria, more than 500 miles away, deep within the American Zone of Occupation. We had all heard that it was one of the nicer camps and I decided it was worth a shot. So, with nothing to my name, I traveled down to Deggendorf.

When I look back on what I thought would have been my triumphant return to Haltern, I was more than naïve. But at the time, there was nothing more for me to have been. I had lost my parents at fourteen and had had nobody to raise me up in the ways of the world. I realize now that my immaturity only served to make my anger even more intense. I am fortunate that I did not kill somebody while I was in Haltern. Add to this my lack of formal education, and I was certainly not very impressive to those I encountered. The only thing I had going for me was that I was smart enough to know that I had a lot of adjusting to do, and a lot to learn as well.

1. Grandfather Alexander Lebenstein.

2. Grandmother Henrietta Lebenstein.

3. Grandfather Alexander Lebenstein's butcher shop at 36 Disselhof
   Strasse. Note the "A. Lebenstein" sign that is hanging over the
   door. The sign is now on display in the rail car on the grounds of
   the Alexander-Lebenstein-Realschule. A young Natan Lebenstein
   is now operating the shop since the death of his father.

4. young Lotte Josephs before her marriage to Natan Lebenstein.

5. Natan and Lotte Lebenstein, undated.

6. Alex as a baby with his mother and three sisters.

7. Alex as a baby.

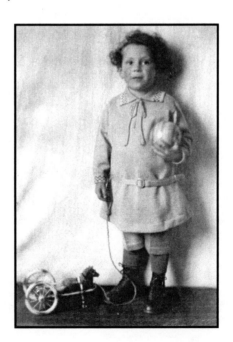

8. Alex as a toddler.

9. Kindergarten 1933. Note the Nazi flags in the rear of the picture and the glum countenance on the faces of all the children with the exception of the curly haired Alex who is clearly mugging for the camera.

10. First day of school.

11. Alex and his parents and two sisters in front of the family garden gazebo.

12. Alex, age 9.

13. Alex "smoking" in his lederhosen.

14. Alex in apron, ready to assist   15. Farm Butcher
    in the butcher shop.

16. Alex the shepherd in the backyard at Disselhof 36. The fence
    in the background is the same fence against which they
    caught their breath and nursed their wounds on the night of
    Kristallnacht

17. Alex with his parents at the time of his Bar Mitzvah while residing in the *Judenhaus*.

18. Six year old Alex in front of the gazebo with sisters Rose (left) and Alice (right) and two neighbors.

19. Disselhof 36, home and butcher shop in happier days.

20. Alex in the family vegetable garden with his sisters

21. . The resulting destruction of the Haltern Synagogue in the aftermath of *Kristallnacht*, November 10, 1938.

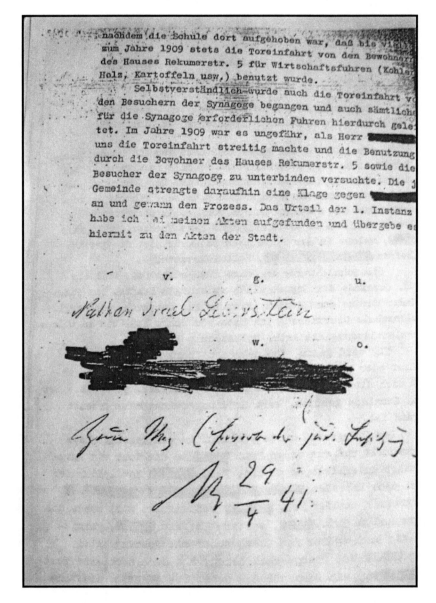

22. Signing over the remaining Jewish property in the City of Haltern on April 29, 1941. This document bears the signature of "Natan Israel Lebenstein." The middle name of "Israel" had been added to the birth certificates of all Jewish men. "Sarah" was added to that of all Jewish women. The signature of the witness has been inked out. This document is still a part of the City Archives.

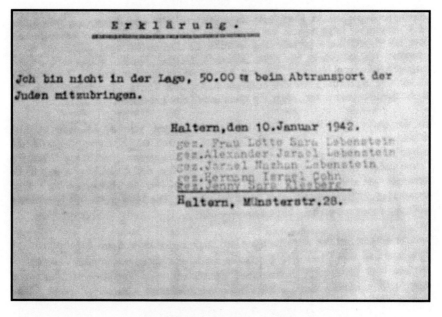

23. The last five remaining Jews residing in Haltern were designated for transport in January, 1942. Unable to pay the individual 50DM fee charged for this service, Natan Lebenstein was directed to the City Hall where his declaration on behalf of himself, his wife Lotte, son Alex, Frau Jenny Kleeberg, and Hermann Cohen was duly noted and recorded for the archives. The signature of the official has also been inked over in this document.

24. An identity again. On 20 September 1945, Alex regained his name and identity. The only difference between this identification card and one issued during the Nazi reign is the absence of the Eagle and Swastika.

25. Alex in the Fall of 1945.

26. Group photo taken in Displaced Persons (DP) Camp Deggendorf.

27. Crazy man in the kitchen, Alex proudly wearing his apron in Camp Deggendorf where he found a niche in the camp kitchen.

28. February, 1947. Alex in the grocery store on Nine Mile Road in
Richmond, VA. With him are his sister Rose and brother-in-law
Edward Spanier, and niece Esther.

PART III

Life Anew

CHAPTER 16

An Identity Again

"I had to come back from the dead."

Shortly after his return to Haltern in August, 1945, Alex Lebenstein went about regaining his identity so that he could begin life anew. On September 20, 1945, Alex was issued new identification papers. Once again he had a name and an identity. For four long years, from ages 14 to 18, he did not officially have a name and had been reduced to a slave labor camp prisoner number that he wore on his chest.

It had been six months since his liberation by the Russians near Danzig. During that time Alex survived a near fatal bout with typhus, the cessation of hostilities in the area, the adventure of the train ride and his journey to the West, all leading to his long anticipated return to Haltern. That odyssey was also filled with the disappointments of the more certain loss of his mother, his home, as well as the ugly reception of some of the townspeople. The sojourn towards recovery continued with his decision not to re-claim German citizenship but rather to accept the status of a displaced person (DP). His next stop: The DP Camp located in Deggendorf, Bavaria.

The Deggendorf DP camp, a former Wehrmacht training academy and headquarters, boasted better housing than almost all of the camps in the Zones of Occupation. It even had a swimming pool. This was in sharp contrast to many of the DP camps being occupied by Jews and other displaced persons which had formerly been slave labor or even concentration camps.

I told the people at City Hall they knew who I was, they still had my birth certificate, and I demanded my papers. While I was probably far more surly and rude than I needed to be, I did not feel like they were doing me any great favors by simply providing me with something I was legally entitled to have in my possession. My birth certificate was brought from the archives, and I noted that it had been altered a couple of times. They had added "Israel" as a middle name, as was required of all Jewish men during the Nazi regime. It also reported that I had been deported to Riga in January, 1942. If nothing else, the Nazis had been extremely thorough in documenting everything during their reign of terror. The only thing that made my new identification card different from those that were issued during the Nazi era was the absence of the Nazi eagle and swastika. It was exactly the same card and format that they had been issuing during those years.

Sadly, nothing really changed for me. I did not feel empowered nor did it allow me any additional privileges. In the fall of 1945, the entire country was largely a refugee camp. Death and destruction were still everywhere. Entire towns lay in ruin, and while the Allies were doing what they could to restore order, it was still mass chaos. With my newly acquired identification card, I was merely one rung higher on the ladder now.

Obtaining my identification card made me feel whole again, no more, no less. It was no different a feeling than what you would feel if you were on vacation and had lost your wallet, credit cards, and passport, and then finally had had them replaced. You do not have any greater status than before; you are merely equal to where you had been. In my case, the degradation and dehumanization had ceased, but my mental state was not significantly better. At last I was a free human being with a name again; not a slave or merely a faceless number to be ordered about.

I visited Haltern one more time during my stay at Deggendorf, but things had not changed appreciably, and as a result, I closed that chapter of my life. I vowed that I would never return to Haltern again.

I saw many people still essentially trapped in displaced persons camps. Those poor people were often stuck behind the same barbed wire that had incarcerated them for so many years. The only thing that made it better was that the Allies and the Joint Distribution Committee (JDC) attempted to make these camps more habitable. They improved sanitary conditions and provided much needed food and clothing, medical care, and other supplies. Children could resume [or in some cases begin] their educations. Trades were taught, and normal signs and activities of life began anew. Marriages were performed and children were born. What were absent in these former prison camps were the roll calls, the beatings, and the smoke coming from the chimneys of the crematoria. Within the camps there was an internal governing body of residents that naturally evolved from the ranks of those who possessed formal education and leadership skills. It was this governing body that would request everything from topcoats to keep people warm to food and medical supplies to keep them fed and get them well. While the barracks were the same, conditions were definitely better. They also managed a search committee to help people try to find relatives in Europe as well as abroad. But nobody could help me find my mother.

CHAPTER 17

Crazy Man in the Kitchen

"After my experiences in the camps, I was very selfish; I didn't say thank you and was more intent on grabbing what was mine."

With the fall of the Third Reich, much of Europe was in ruins. City after city were now piles of rubble. The firebombing of Dresden, immortalized by Kurt Vonnegut in his novel <u>Slaughterhouse Five</u>, killed more people than the atomic bombing of Hiroshima. Cities dating back to Roman times, with histories of a thousand years or longer, were destroyed.

This decimation also meant that over eleven million Europeans remained without a home, and often times without a country. Having been uprooted by the Nazis during the war, these displaced persons, or DPs, needed to be taken care of in the short term and to have assistance provided them if they were to survive the long term. Because of the manner in which the Nazis had continued to close satellite camps in conquered territories in the face of the advancing allies at war's end, seven million of these DPs were located in Germany proper. In addition to no less than 800,000 Poles, there were approximately 225,000 Jews who had been liberated from all of the slave labor and death camps.

The original plan for those who had been displaced by the war was to repatriate them to their countries of origin as soon as possible. Through the efforts of the Allies, and the United Nations Relief and Rehabilitation Administration (UNRRA), which had been founded in November, 1943, in anticipation of these great needs, by the end of 1945 more than six million DPs had already returned to their respective native lands to resume the lives that they had known prior to the war. However, between 1.5 and 2 million of them refused repatriation for a variety of reasons. Many non-Jews in and out of the DP camps did not want to return to their native lands because they feared reprisals for collaboration with the Nazis during occupation, or in other cases, did not look forward to living under totalitarian regimes in what would now be countries located behind the Iron Curtain. The Cold War was in its infancy, but already in the Soviet satellite countries of Eastern Europe (Czechoslovakia, Yugoslavia, Poland, Ukraine) as well as the Baltic States (Latvia, Estonia, Lithuania), there was a growing new order of things, and the opportunities there seemed bleaker than life in the West.

For the Jews who were in the DP camps, there usually was no home to which they could return. If not physically destroyed during Kristallnacht or in subsequent attacks, or by collateral damage during the war proper, there was largely nothing to return home to – no family, no community, no culture. As in the case of Alex's attempt to live in Haltern, they were often greeted with hostility and contempt. After all that these people had endured at the hands of the Nazis, how tragic it was when this continuing contempt sometimes led to the murder of Holocaust survivors by townspeople. Many of the residents of these cities still believed Hitler's maniacal rantings as to how all of the hardships encountered by the German people could be laid at the feet of the Jews.

Deggendorf is a town in Bavaria, the Southeastern portion of Germany, and the capital of the district named Deggendorf. Steeped in history, the earliest traces of settlement are found near the Danube River and date back some 8,000 years. In 1002, Henry II, the Holy Roman Emperor, established his supremacy over the area.

The site of the displaced persons camp was located in a cluster of buildings that were built in 1863 as a hospital. From 1930 until the end of the war, *it was used as barracks for the Wehrmacht and a special military school for Unteroffizieren (junior officers). This came to an end April 27, 1945, when the site was conquered by the 26th Infantry Division, as World War Two was winding down. The displaced persons camp formally came into being at the end of May or the beginning of June.*

At the outset, Deggendorf became home to some 2,000 Jewish refugees, who created a cultural center that included two newspapers, a theatre group, a synagogue, a kosher kitchen, sports teams, and other vestiges of civilization. It was very much a city unto itself. Additionally, residents had the ability to learn a trade, and the children received both general and religious educations. The camp even issued its own currency known as the Deggendorf Dollar. Many of the camp's residents were survivors of the concentration camp at Theresienstadt.

Each resident of the camp was expected to contribute to the general welfare of the displaced persons community. Those with special skills, such as teachers, tailors, cooks, engineers, doctors, would naturally resume working in their chosen vocations. Others would provide labor in and around the camp.

Germany was no longer my home. It was not real to me anymore. Everything that I had known as a child had been ripped away from me and destroyed. I refused the German citizenship that had been re-offered to me. After the manner in which it had been stripped away from my parents and me, I could not imagine ever wanting to be a German citizen again. After witnessing the barbaric treatment experienced by my father, who had been a proud German Jew, there was no way that I could ever conceive of carrying a German passport again.

I took the train from northwestern Germany down to the southeastern state of Bavaria, arriving in Deggendorf ready to start a better life. I had one suitcase with very little in it, plus the clothes on my back. Whatever new life I was heading to, I was certainly doing it with a minimum of possessions. Armed with my new identity card, processing into the camp was relatively easy, and I was assigned a place to sleep. I shared a room with two other men at first. Their names were Peter Klages and Artie Graboschewsky. A roof over my head, a bed to sleep in with clean blankets and sheets, now physically healthy, in clothes that fit me, and with sufficient food, I slept well and was grateful to be among my fellow survivors.

However, even after being in the DP Camp at Deggendorf for quite a while, the fear of being selected out and shot was still very much a part of me. Some of these old habits engrained over many years are still with me to this very day.

In Deggendorf I was channeling my anger and hostility by training in the classroom to join the *Hagganah* in Palestine. The *Hagganah* and *Irgun* were underground fighting units organized to promote the birth of a Jewish homeland, and if necessary, to fight against the British who controlled the region and opposed Jewish settlement there. It was ironic that my two sisters had escaped to England prior to the war, and the British were part of the Allied team that had helped to win the war and liberate many of my brothers and sisters from concentration camps. Yet now, they were becoming my enemy, a target of the venom that coursed through my veins.

Another means by which I channeled my anger was in pursuit of physical activities. Soccer was one such pursuit, but I had also discovered boxing. Sometimes I wished that I had not. There was one match against a very large man when I was repeatedly knocked down. Even though it was all supposed to be in fun, and we were wearing the big boxing gloves, he took it far more seriously than I did. It may have been because I was such a wise guy, and he figured that I needed to be taken down a notch or two. Well, the man was an absolute mountain, and he pummeled me. The next day, one of my eyes was barely open. So much for any career I may have been contemplating in professional boxing.

I had been just a kid when snatched away from life, and had no particular skill to offer, so I did what I could, and was always willing to lend a hand. This led to a variety of menial tasks and assignments. My first assignment in the camp was as one of the gate guards. Rather than guarding prisoners in the camp, our job was to keep order at the gate. As such, it was our responsibility to insure that anyone attempting to gain entrance into the facility had a legitimate reason for being there. This could range from looking for a loved one to seeking shelter. We were also charged with directing visitors in need of fresh clothing to the place where they could replace garments that may have been infested with lice or communicable diseases to keep the camp inhabitants free of these horrible diseases. It was also our responsibility to insure that undesirables, e.g. Nazis and people who would do us harm, did not gain entrance to the camp. I did this for only a very short while because it quickly became very evident to those in authority that I was simply too openly hostile to everyone around me to even perform the simple task of keeping the gate.

I was shortly thereafter reassigned to duties in the camp kitchen. One of the things I attempted to do was to ensure that the food was both tasty and plentiful. After what all of us had been through, food had once again become a source of enjoyment and a real priority in our lives. While the Joint Distribution Committee (the "Joint") and camp administration was pretty good at getting us what we needed and wanted, from time to time I would go out into the countryside and buy fresh chicken, butter, eggs, and milk from some of the local farmers. Most of them were more than happy to part with these foodstuffs in exchange for some hard cash. One particular farmer, however, was a real pain in the neck, and would often tell me that he had nothing to sell. I suspected that he was still an ardent Nazi and he knew the provisions were for hungry Jews so he would often hand me this line. After several refusals on his part to sell us anything from his farm and knowing that he later sold things to other people, I decided that he was going to make a contribution to the camp whether he wanted to or not.

Even with the best efforts of the Joint, fresh meat was difficult to obtain. So, one day I took it upon myself to pay this particular farmer's place a little visit, and I took one of his dairy cows. Actually, the cow just sort of followed me home to the camp. Ha! To make sure that we would not be discovered, we walked in the stream that also ran through the camp so that nobody could track our footprints. This was a very smart cow! With the help of several of the other men, we grabbed some ropes and used one of the trees to put together the necessary rigging in order to slaughter the cow. We ate well in the days to come. I made sure that we used every bit of that cow. Every part was a delicacy, even the organ meats. As this was a dairy cow, I remember how yellow the fat was that we used for different preparations. The bones and meat scraps went into a delicious soup with the barley that was readily available.

One day I was working in the kitchen when my new friend Marianne Mayer showed up with some friends of hers, sixteen-year-old

Eva Goldsmith (now Borel), her mother and brother. They were a family of three who needed a place and wanted to stay together if possible. However, the camp was full to capacity at this point. Marianne had come to me to see if I could find them such a place within the camp because I had a reputation as a guy who could get things done. I knew of an outbuilding that they could use and remain together. It was an empty building that needed cleaning. I knew where to get mattresses, a table and chairs, and other necessities. Toilet facilities were there and useable. I cleaned and furnished the place to the best of my ability. The Goldsmith family was grateful to have a place to live. A few days passed, when Eva came storming angrily into the kitchen. She immediately started beating my chest with her little fists and was screaming, "Why did you do this? What did you do to us?" Apparently she had just learned the little secret that I had opted not to disclose to her and her family. Their quarters had been the camp's morgue when under the control of the *Wehrmacht*. She has long since forgiven me, and we are still the best of friends.

As the months passed by, I participated in more and more of the activities that the camp had to offer. We were of course free to go into town for movies, meals, and anything else that struck our fancy. At one point I even volunteered to be a stagehand in a performance of an operetta within the camp entitled *Im Weissen Roszal am Wolfgangs See* (In the White Little Horse on Wolfgangs Sea).

After years of being deprived of close contact and intimacy, one of the pleasures within Deggendorf was certainly that of dancing and companionship. One night, I had escorted Eva to the movies in town, and we were walking back to camp, in anticipation of attending a late evening party. All of a sudden, out of nowhere, we were attacked. Because it was raining hard, we were huddled together under a large umbrella which allowed them to sneak up behind us. I was hit from behind so hard that I spun around and was knocked cold. Fortunately, I was not out long, because the downpour had flooded the deep gutters, and I was revived by the flowing water in which I had landed face down. Bleeding from a severe gash inside my lip (a scar that I bear to this day) I ran back to the little archway in the wall to which these obviously drunken American soldiers had dragged Eva. The troops were drunk enough to have done something pretty stupid in attacking me, and they were all attempting to compound their idiocy by fondling her. I don't know what their intentions were, but I was not waiting to find out. With a rage and fury that came from deep inside me, I roared and promptly cold cocked two of them by knocking their heads together. The others ran off. I took Eva to the party that we had planned on attending. I was soaking wet, and the blood all over my face and shirt made my injuries look worse than they were. But the experience served to place me back on guard and to recognize that we were still not completely safe. That was probably the worst experience that I endured while at Deggendorf, but by and large, it was a very good place for me, and for nearly all of the displaced persons who came through there en route to new lives in other places.

Deggendorf was the place in which I regained my physical strength. I put on more weight and genuinely felt much better. It was also good to be in the company of others, strangers just the day before, but friends today, hoping to build new lives just like me.

It seemed no matter where I was in the concentration camps and also here, there were older people, with maturity, that I looked up to for support and advice. Always being the youngest wherever I was in some ways a benefit to me. There were still good people who cared for others. Of course, there were others who were only out for themselves. I guess it was this often very strong contrast in people and their values that was so difficult for me, previously a basically trusting person, to accept. After my experiences in the camps, I was very selfish; I didn't say thank you and was more intent on grabbing what was mine.

I should probably relate to those of you who are taking the time to read this story a more humorous episode that also took place in Deggendorf. From the time that I was a little boy, my mother always restricted me to eating only one-half of an egg at a time. It did not matter how old I was or what meal we were eating, it was only one-half egg. While it may have been a shortage of eggs, my suspicion is that it really stemmed from an old wives' tale that my mother had heard and embraced about boys and eggs. Who knows for sure what went through her mind. To this day I don't know why I could never have more than one-half of an egg. Ironically, all of my sisters were allowed to eat one or more eggs whenever they wanted. As I got older and was starving in the camps, I resolved that one day if I were ever free to do so, I would eat an entire pan, containing at least a dozen eggs, all by myself. I imagined how good they would taste and how wonderful it would be to absolutely gorge myself on them. I can remember many a time when I would go to sleep dreaming about my pan of eggs.

So, while I was in the DP Camp in Deggendorf, dealing with store owners, negotiating with farmers and other locals, I got hold of a dozen farm fresh eggs as well as some freshly churned butter, and I cooked them all up. One by one, I cracked the shells and dropped the eggs into the butter that was sizzling and crackling. And then, after I had cooked them just the way I like them, I sat down with a big spoon and started shoveling them into my mouth. Oh, how wonderful they tasted… at the beginning. After a quick start, I was soon slowing down when I realized that my eyes and my dreams may have been bigger than my stomach. Soon I found myself having to force them down to keep the promise I had made to myself, and I got desperately sick. We didn't know from salmonella or anything at that time, but I was sick for a good day or two after that. I don't know if it was the dozen eggs, the rich butter, or the combination of the two, but I surely paid the price for my gluttony. Today I love eggs, but definitely in moderation. Two at a time is plenty for me.

CHAPTER 18

Lost and Found

"We didn't talk about the pain. We remembered what happened and celebrated our close calls and our survival; all the while, we dealt with the conflicting guilt associated with our survival."

Ernie Pyle had been an American journalist who became one of America's first war correspondents of World War II. Instead of the traditional reporting of battles or the activities of the highly visible brass, Pyle wrote about the war from the perspective of the common foot soldier. This earned him the popularity and respect of all ranks within the military and culminated in his being awarded the Pulitzer Prize in 1944. He is credited with getting soldiers awarded combat pay through the impact of a column that he wrote urging the additional compensation. He was killed on April 18, 1945, while accompanying elements of the Marine Corps 6th Marine Division, on the island of Iejima, an island off the Okinawa Honto coast. His body was so riddled by Japanese machine gun fire that identification was possible only through his dog tags. He was buried at the National Memorial Cemetery of the Pacific at Punchbowl on the island of Oahu, Hawaii. His abrupt and tragic death prompted an outpouring of public support and a clamoring for recognition and honors. The christening of this troop transport in his name was just one of many honors afforded to him by a grateful nation and public. After the war, this ship brought many displaced persons to the United States during the time that it was kept in service.

I was slowly beginning a new life in Deggendorf. I made new friends. We remembered what happened and celebrated our close calls and our survival; all the while, we dealt with the conflicting guilt associated with our survival.

Feeling better and better each day, I would occasionally think about my sisters, but for whatever reason, did not desire contact with them. I am led to believe that this was normal behavior for someone in my position. My anger with my sisters had not abated because in my mind they could or should have done more for me and my parents. Looking back in hindsight, I know that I had behaved more like a child than an adult. I also realize that they had themselves barely gotten out of Germany, and it was as much my parents' fault for not leaving, one way or another, if not more. The time to have left Germany was in fact when my sisters left. By staying and naively believing that things would get better or return to normal, my father sealed our fates.

I have a flashback to early 1937 and a confrontation between my father and my uncle Jacob Meyers, a well-to-do butcher in nearby Bochum. He came to persuade my parents to let him arrange their immigration to join him in Bogata, Colombia. He had purchased modern sausage-making and other equipment with his son Ernie, and planned to open a meat factory there. I remember well when my uncle extended the invitation to my father, for his expertise, to partner with him in this new venture. But my father was afraid of making any change and refused the offer. I can only wonder how different our life would have been had my father accepted this gracious offer.

In any event, my sister, Alice, was still in England, when she discovered my name on a list of survivors. She in turn contacted my sister, Rose, who by this time, had settled with her husband, Edward Spanier, in Richmond, Virginia, in the United States.

In the Fall of 1946, about a year after I had arrived in Deggendorf I heard from my sister Rose via the phone in the camp office. She informed me that now it was time for us to be together.

We began an exchange of letters, the three of us, and while it was good to hear from my sisters, it also stirred up a great number of mixed feelings within me.

My niece, Esther (now Binshtok), later confirmed for me that her mother, Rose Spanier, had told her directly that whenever my sisters had asked my parents about leaving Germany they had always refused. So, as I said, it was probably even more my parents' fault that we endured what we did based on their ill-fated decisions, rather than a lack of desire on the part of one or both of my sisters to assist us.

There has been a great deal of speculation in my family as to why my parents did not leave Germany. Obviously, at first it was because they sincerely believed that we would be okay where we were. As I have said before, my father was a loyal German Jew, who had fought bravely for the Fatherland in the First World War. By the time he probably realized that things would not be improving, it was too late. The next issue surely was that my parents did not have the means with which to leave the country. My mother was actually the money manager of the family. Some people have suggested that, given the dire straits we were in, my parents should have borrowed or found the money necessary to flee the country, even if it meant defaulting on these loans. I know that because of the high code of honor by which my parents both lived, particularly my father with his background as a soldier, that this too was not an option. They had taught me well that people of honor do not lie or cheat. I also know that both of them would rather die than break their word. But speaking to Rose from Deggendorf, I was still acting more like the eleven year old child rather than the nineteen year old man.

I then informed my sister that I was preparing myself to go to Palestine, to serve in the *Hagganah* and help secure an independent nation state for the Jewish people. No sooner had I said my piece, than Rose informed me in no uncertain terms that my place was to come to the U.S. in order that we could be together. When I resisted and repeated that I wanted to go to Palestine, she told me that I would come to see her first. As my older sister, she insisted that I must respect her wishes, and then, after a visit, I could go on to Palestine if that was still my desire.

Time passed and we were informed by sources in Palestine that they had neither housing nor enough food for us to come over there. Also, it was rumored that there were negotiations under way whereby Britain might agree to give up a part of their mandate in Palestine to create a homeland for us. At the same time, people were beginning to leave Deggendorf. I became restless too. This restlessness and the uncertainty about my future with the *Hagganah* made me reluctantly accept my sister's offer to arrange sponsorship papers that would grease the skids for me to get into the United States for the desired visit.

I let the camp leadership know that my sister and brother-in-law were working on the papers, and that I would be leaving shortly. Months went by without any progress. Letters from the camp to my family inquiring as to progress on my papers went unanswered. In a selfish, smart way, I believe that my brother-in-law was stalling to prevent me from coming over.

There was also a system within the camp that awarded us "points" for the amount of labor we provided. This was in addition to the regular camp money and allowance that we received. These points helped you establish credentials for yourself, so that if you did not have family that could vouch for you and assure the American authorities that you would not become a burden on the state, the Joint Committee would make this representation on your behalf and assume any liability for you.

Finally, I had been at Deggendorf long enough, had worked hard enough to impress the leadership, and to earn enough points so that I no longer needed my family to sponsor my travel to the United States. So I worked with the camp authorities, completed my application, and it was approved. When I informed my family that I had obtained a guarantee from the Committee, bingo, the next week my family-sponsored papers arrived from the U.S. I opted to use this set of papers with which to enter the U.S. because this freed up a spot for someone else for the Committee to sponsor and that was okay with me. All of these formalities were completed by the Committee, and I was soon on my way.

I started the paperwork process that would allow me to go to the United States. First, there was an interview at the American Consulate in Munich, followed by a medical examination. Soon thereafter, I received notice that my visa was ready, and that I would be departing after the first of the year, traveling by ship from Bremen to the Port of New York.

We left Deggendorf in December 1946 for our trip to America. We were trucked to the train station where we were placed aboard a passenger train to Bremen. This port city, located on the Northwestern coast of Germany, was, along with Bremerhaven, under American control even though the whole of Northern Germany was actually occupied by the British. These harbor areas were serving as major logistical support centers for all of the American troops stationed in Germany, as well as assembly areas and embarkation points for thousands of displaced persons emigrating to the United States. After your arrival, your wait inside the center could be a day or a week, depending on availability of ships in the harbor.

When it was time for us to go, we were fed an early morning breakfast, and taken to a nearby railroad siding. After a short train ride to the pier, we were able to gaze upon the ship that would transport us to the United States: the *SS Ernie Pyle*.

This ship was named after the famous war correspondent who himself had recently died while in combat with troops in the Pacific. We boarded in early January, 1947. I remember walking up the gangplank very full of misgivings and wondering what exactly I was getting myself into by agreeing to go to America. I did not know the language or the customs and had virtually no money except the ten dollars that had been given to me by the JDC. It truly was the beginning of a new year and a new life.

As we boarded the ship, we were directed by the ship's officers and crew exactly where to find our sleeping quarters. The men were berthed on one side of the ship, the women on the other. All of the rooms were full of bunk beds, much like army barracks, but very comfortable. Being a troop ship, there were no portholes where we slept, and so for many people, this presented a very confining feeling.

I also remember being exposed to white bread for the first time, and wondering, "What the hell is this?" Warm from the oven, I didn't know what it was. It certainly was not cake and surely did not resemble anything I had ever seen before. Even in the DP camp we did not have it. It was the first time that I had ever seen something in this shape. And it was so white! And full of air holes! It was very strange indeed.

Overall though, the food was very good. But then again, my standards had been so low for so many years, that I was just grateful to have food in my stomach.

We were aboard for twelve days rather than the eight or nine days as scheduled, because we encountered horrible storms that continually pushed us back. I was fine the entire time aboard ship, but there were certainly a whole lot of folks who were not. I would say that probably ninety- nine percent of the passengers were sick, but not me. The worst part was the stink from the vomit. It was everywhere.

The women moaned, "I can't take it anymore," and begged for help. So I would suggest going up on deck. Then it would be a matter of putting one of them on my back and climbing the iron ladder with her like a backpack. We would no sooner get up on deck and she would spy the ocean and the wave action, and up would come anything that she had in her stomach. Then the moaning began again about how it was worse up on top and the begging continued anew to take her back down. So again, on my back, like a backpack, down the iron ladder, one rung at a time, all the while I am praying that she would not vomit all over me! Then the next one would want to try it. Two or three different ones would ask me every day. It was like my daily workout. I could have been a member of the crew. Up and down, up and down.

Obviously one of the more memorable events of my transit across the ocean occurred one night out on the fantail of the ship. I was out on the fantail on one of the nights that the storms were not raging and had ducked into this little locker where they stored a large coil of rope, simply to get out of the wind. I was enjoying a cigarette when this rather good looking young woman came up. I had not seen her before, but that did not stop me from inviting her in out of the wind, and offering her a cigarette. We talked for about an hour, and then we started doing some smooching. One thing led to another, and pretty soon we were meeting one another's needs. Oh how nice it was to simply spend time with a woman in a relaxed setting. Even though we were housed with men on one side of the ship and women on the other, sex was rampant anyway. Let's face it, for years we had all been deprived by opportunity and most had had their libido greatly diminished by a lack of food and energy. Once liberation happened and everyone was feeling better, sex was everywhere. It was also the reason that there were so many children born in DP camps, and also the reason that Jewish couples started having children immediately after being married. Part of it was pure lust, but also because we all felt a tremendous obligation, if not even a burden, to start re-building our people, and to start replacing all those who had been exterminated in the camps. Another reason is that we were all seeking closeness and following human instinct. It was not a matter of moral versus immoral; it was a matter of comfort and survival. It was more emotional than physical. It was about merely expressing long buried emotions. Protection was not thought about, and really was not around any way.

I had a similar experience on the overnight train ride from Deggendorf to Bremen. It was another cattle car, but obviously we were not packed in as we had been when we were being transported by the Nazis. Candidly, I was young, had healthy urges, and like other men, this was another way that we exerted our control and felt like conquerors. I am also sure that we were probably acting out because of the manner in which we had all been held in subservience for so many years. I don't know for sure. I guess it was another opportunity to be free and a big shot.

While we were sailing over, I had resolved that I would give America a try, and if it was to my liking, that I would stay. If it was not, well, I guess I had the option of going to Palestine or finding another place that I could build a new life. I was still in contact with my friend, Ewald Aul, as well as other people from the DP camp.

When we pulled into New York Harbor on January 16, 1947, we were all anxious to get off of the ship. Fortunately, our papers had been checked while in transit, so when we docked it was simply a matter of walking off of the ship and down the gangplank. Obviously none of us had anything to declare with Customs. The big concern to the officials was simply whether we were entering the country legally. If we had our green card, we were set to go.

Many of the people on the ship were intrigued or even excited by the sight of the Statue of Liberty. I did not know anything about it. With only three years of education, and nothing that would have allowed me to know otherwise, I simply saw it as another big statue. It made no real impression on me. Now, today, as a very proud American citizen, I appreciate daily the great values for which it stands.

CHAPTER 19

Land of Plenty

"Am I White?"

On January 16, 1947, the SS Ernie Pyle steamed into New York Harbor, past the Statue of Liberty, carrying among its passengers, nineteen year old Alexander Lebenstein. He was greeted in New York by his sister Rose's husband, Edward Spanier. Rose had stayed behind in Richmond, Virginia to continue to operate the grocery store that the family owned on Nine Mile Road and to care for their two-year-old daughter Esther.

I had fully expected that my sister Rose would come to New York to meet my ship, and to pick me up. After all, it had been over seven years since we had last seen one another. Sadly, my brother-in-law, Edward, came alone. With Rose, he too had escaped to England where he continued to romance my sister as he had been doing in Germany when the family was all together. I do not remember who sponsored them in their move to the United States in 1942. I do know that they first lived in Akron, Ohio, before eventually ending up in Richmond, Virginia.

At first I did not believe that Rose had not accompanied Edward to New York, and I kept looking behind the pillars and posts and buildings, suspecting that she was hiding like we had done as children, and that she was going to spring out at any second and attack me with hugs and kisses. Edward would then say something like, "Alex, she is not here. Rose is back in Richmond. You will see her when we get there later." That was very painful for me and it also angered me in some ways. Again, my emotions were so sensitive and close to the surface.

Because it was January, the days were short, and so by four o'clock, it was already starting to get dark. The bright lights, making nighttime seem like daytime, as well as the hustle and bustle of New York City at night, was beyond anything that I had ever experienced in my life. The sights, the sounds, the smells, it was enough to put me in a state of sensory overload. One could feel very alive simply by walking the streets. It was now well after five o'clock, yet the stores were still open and full of people. Wow. If this was America, it truly was something!

While we were passing the time waiting for the train that would take us to Richmond, we took the bus down to 42nd Street, which of course was even brighter and more animated with people. I was more than content with simply walking the streets of New York and attempting to soak it all in. What an incredible land this America! No wonder it had the capability and industrial might to beat Hitler at his own game.

One place that we absolutely had to go in and look around was the Planter's Peanut Store. The giant peanut man was actually a roasting machine in the window, shaking back and forth. The smell of roasting peanuts was all over the street. My love for peanuts had not diminished over the years. Because of my excitement at seeing this store, my brother-in-law bought me a small bag of peanuts. What a treat they were. Hot, fresh, well roasted peanuts and I could eat the entire bag right then and there if I wanted. What I could not get over was the fact that people were eating their peanuts and throwing their shells into the gutter and on the sidewalk. That would never have happened in Germany. I protested to my brother-in-law, and he was quick to tell me to do the same thing so that I would fit in. "Throw them in the street like everyone else," he commanded. I guess I did, but it certainly felt strange to do so. I had every expectation to have put the shells in a separate bag or even in to my pocket. This was all very strange to me.

We left for Richmond by train from Penn Station that same evening. The train ride was uneventful, and we arrived in Richmond in the wee hours of the morning.

I had no sooner gotten off the train and into the station when I noticed a sign over the water fountain and another on the benches. Not reading English, I could not understand what they were attempting to convey. "Only for white people," is what Edward translated for me.

Imagine my shock and dismay to see at the drinking fountains evidence that America was not the land of freedom that I thought it was. Instead of signs that said *Juden Verboten* (Jews forbidden), I was greeted with signs that prohibited all but white people from drinking or eating, and more signs that did not allow them to sit on benches also reserved for use by only white people. My amazement continued as we traveled from the train station via bus to the Spanier home. I would learn that black people were required to sit in the back of the bus. I learned this when I sat down in a seat just past the middle and was directed rather harshly by the bus driver to move to another seat closer to the front of the bus. I had opted for the other seat because only aisle seats were open, and I wanted to sit near a window so that I could see the city. The driver was adamant that I sit where he indicated. His attitude scared me because of the authoritarian tone in his voice. It was the same tone that the Nazis had used so many years ago before the war when we were directed when and where we could walk or shop. My English consisted of "hello" and "goodbye," and I could count to ten. I did not know what to believe. The minimal education that I had received as a child had obviously not included anything about American history. As a result, I had no idea that there had been a Civil War or slavery, or that this racial intolerance existed so strongly, especially in the South, where we now were. I had seen no similar signs in New York, so this very much confused me.

What really confused me was what it meant to be white. Were people marked by color in America? White, yellow, green... green card. It seemed that color was everywhere and everything. The big question in my mind was "What am I now?" Before liberation, I was only a number, but what am I now?" I had just gone through a process of degradation and discrimination simply for being Jewish. I found myself wondering, what color am I? Do I pass? Am I white? Edward assured me, "*Du bist ein Weisser*" ("You are white"). It didn't happen all at one time, but I learned slowly about slavery, the manner in which the issue had split the country, and how the Civil War had been fought over it, and how in parts of the country, it was still being fought on a daily basis.

The bus took us to the grocery store above which they lived, and I remember my sister, Rose, coming down the stairs to greet me warmly, but not in the manner that I had built up in my mind. It never really occurred to me that my sister would now be married, committed to another person, and have a two year old daughter of her own, my niece, Esther. I guess part of me had assumed that our loving sibling relationship would be like it had been before she left home. I was still very much in my own childhood mind. I guess it was for that reason that it was so shocking to look up the stairs to see baby Esther, in a diaper, looking down at me from behind the spindles of the banister, giggling and wiggling as only toddlers can. Sweet and adorable, she warmed to me almost immediately. It was wonderful to be around a baby so full of innocence and joy.

Literally within only a couple of hours of arrival, it was time to open the store downstairs. I soon found myself wearing a grocer's apron, and doing things as directed. I could not understand the language, so I was dependent upon them to tell me what to do in German. I was already determined to learn English as soon as possible and to forget everything German. I hated everything about Germany at that point and did not attempt to hide it.

To this end, I deliberately tried to forget the German language. I did not want to read, hear, or speak it -- even though it was my native language, my culture, my heritage, I was just so angry and filled with hate that I did not want to have anything to do with it. Now I usually equate the use of the word "hate" with dogs, and use "dislike" with people. At that point in my life, it was still very much hate for all that was German. My sister and brother-in-law could not understand why I felt this way. But then again, why should they? They had not lived through what I had endured all those years. They were either in England or the United States.

They were inquisitive about the fate of our parents and politely interested in what had happened to me during these treacherous times. But I noticed that there were no tears shed by them, no depth of feelings, only the reaction of someone who is listening to a very sad story that really did not personally impact them. As time passed, it became more and more apparent to me that I was nothing more than a burden to them.

As the months passed, I would fight with my family when they spoke German, especially to me. They did not understand how very much I wanted to learn English and to forget about being a German. I would constantly be asking them what the German word they used was, in English, so that I could learn the language. I had no desire to be bilingual or to maintain any of my cultural roots.

The first time I ever observed black people was when I was a small boy back in Haltern. These truly African people were actually part of a circus display portraying them as animals of the wild, complete with the oversized discs in their mouths that served to permanently stretch and disfigure their features. They would walk alongside a cage with a wild animal, such as a tiger in it, and were instructed to act like wild animals themselves by roaring and thrashing with their arms.

In 1947, African-Americans were referred to as "colored" people. This was something else to which I had to become accustomed. The entire white and colored battle left me very confused. I was equally concerned by how seemingly callous and uncaring my own family had become in terms of degrading the black community that their store served. They acted as if they believed the "colored" people were inferior to them. This was both confusing and alarming to me, especially after what I had been through. I wondered if it was ignorance or a lack of knowledge on their part that allowed them to fall into this trap.

They would point out that blacks were not trying to advance themselves, and they would warn me to "watch" certain "colored" people when they came into the store to insure that they did not steal anything. Or they would label this one as a "good one" because he paid his bills on time, or that she was still in school. These distinctions were never made with white people who might frequent the store. About ninety percent of the patrons of the store were "colored."

I was most amazed that my sister and her husband did not view their actions as prejudice, but rather simply a fact of life that they had come to accept in their new homeland. In Europe it was the gypsies that were the thieves; over here in the States, it was the blacks. I always questioned why. Is it because of their color that they are not honest? Nobody could ever give me a satisfactory answer to my questions. Of course I realize now the reason was that there was no good answer to explain their behavior except that they had brought discrimination with them from Europe. It was just flat out wrong of them to prejudge someone solely on the basis of his color or ethnicity, just as the Nazis had done to us because we were Jewish. It took me a long time to figure this out on my own.

I had to ask myself if America and Germany were really so different. Slavery is slavery, oppression is oppression, and intolerance is intolerance. What had I gotten myself into by coming to America? Again, I felt uncertain and confused. Maybe I should just say goodbye and be on my way to Palestine.

I would soon learn another lesson from the school of hard knocks, the importance of having to earn my own way in life. Until then I had either been my parents' perfect little boy or had been assigned work and fed in the various concentration, slave labor, and displaced person camps. I had never really given much thought to the concept of being self-sufficient and paying my own way. Even in Deggendorf we had been afforded a small allowance of Deggendorf dollars that enabled us to shop at the commissary or even in town. I guess this was another way in which my development had been stunted during the previous eight years.

So, here I was working in the store for my sister and brother-in-law and at this point, I was simply doing as I was told. If this meant getting up early to go to the market to pick up meat with Edward, that is what I would do. I really did not think about what I was doing. In some ways, it was the same sort of existence I had experienced in the camps without the obvious pain, degradation, and horrible living conditions of the Nazi regime. I would load, unload, mop and clean, and when I did not know how to do something, Edward would show me. My goal was to make myself useful to them. Nonetheless, I realized that the store was not large enough to support me as well as their family. I must say that during the time I was with my sister and brother-in-law they did buy me a suit and a pair of shoes that allowed me to attend synagogue and other social events.

Looking back, I acknowledge that everyone was struggling to make something for themselves, and Edward and Rose were no exception. My brother-in-law helped me find a job at a supermarket in the Churchill neighborhood where they were in need of a helper. He recommended me to the owner, and I was hired. However, I still lived with my family above their store for a short while.

After saving a few dollars, I moved to a rooming house in South Richmond and found a job as a butcher's helper at an A&P store. Finally, I was on my own in Richmond. I still saw my family, but it was clear to me that they could not comprehend the horror that I had lived through in the course of seven years. While it was never said, I knew that my very being here in Richmond was a burden to them. I realized that it was only a matter of time before I would leave Richmond to strike out on my own and to become an American citizen.

CHAPTER 20

Faith Restored

"Just what I had seen was enough to make me question where God could be and how he could have allowed this to happen. We were the chosen people? Having watched the degradation that was inflicted on my father, I could not reconcile my faith."

From the time that Alex left Richmond in 1947 in search of his own identity, a career, a family, a new country, his was a very typical story for an immigrant who had survived the horrors of the Holocaust. With a decided lack of education, no recognizable skills, limited language ability, it was only through dogged determination to be a good citizen, a hard worker, and a solid family man, that Alex was able to achieve success. However, this success was tempered by the unaddressed anger, distrust, and emotional wounds that continued to fester for nearly fifty years.

As I married, had a family, and built a career and eventually my own business, I was aware that my life was still being impacted by the lasting effects of the anger that continued to live on inside of me. In hindsight, I was probably sterner with my sons than I needed to be, but I think that is a relatively prevalent issue among survivors and their children. In my opinion, most of the second generation, i.e. the children of survivors, have been impacted by our experiences. I would even go so far as to say that consciously or subconsciously the children of survivors probably to some degree resent the impact of the Holocaust on their lives.

I was also quite aware of just how angry I was with God; I did not get back into religious observance until I was married. My wife's family would not have permitted us to marry otherwise. Just what I had seen was enough to make me question where God could be and how he could have allowed all that I had witnessed and endured to have happened. We were the chosen people? Having watched the degradation that was inflicted on my father, I could not reconcile my faith. This was my great dilemma, but it was at this time that I realized that I would owe it to my sons David and Danny to have faith and determined later, as they prepared themselves for *Bar Mitzvah*, that I would prepare myself as well for this auspicious event.

It was up to me to provide for my little family, and I was willing to work long hours every day. All the while, I still found the time to study for my American citizenship. I was proud to be part of the swearing-in ceremony that occurred on April 7, 1953 at the Miami Courthouse. It was a great day for me. I was a citizen again, and a citizen of the best country in the world – the United States of America. I was determined to be 100% American in the same manner as my father had been a proud and loyal German.

It was also at this time that we opted to relocate to New York City, and to buy a co-op apartment in Flushing, Queens. The advantages to this move included a large Jewish community, the opportunity to join a Conservative synagogue, and for David to be entered into Hebrew School. It was during this time that I was really wrestling with my own personal faith. What was I to do? My faith had been so severely defeated by the events that had robbed me of a simple but pleasant life and forced me to endure a version of hell on earth. So, I reaffirmed my decision that it was only proper that I learn along with my sons. I also realized that something was missing from my life, and I was eager to explore what it could be. I was also hungry for education of all kinds.

Because of the heat of the summer in New York City and because this was long before anyone had air conditioning, I would send my family out of the city for the summer, usually up to the Catskill Mountains. We created many wonderful memories in the *Kochalaine* (bungalows with cooking kitchens) favored by many Jews at this time. I would stay in town, working four and half days, and then join them for the weekends.

I would show up with the leftover meat that we couldn't sell by Friday, as well as ice cold fresh fruit, including watermelon, and I would be very popular with the kids. I got permission to leave work a little early on Friday, and even with traffic, I could have a nice barbeque going for everyone on Friday night. As I drove up, the entire colony of kids stormed me, led by my own two boys, knowing that there was going to be something good for everyone to enjoy. I cut up the melon on the old ping pong table, and the kids would line up to get a chunk of it. Even today, this story is being retold by Ronnie and Sandra, the children of my fellow survivor Max Tepper. They still call me "Uncle Alex" to this day. They gleefully share these memories with their own children. It pleases me that I can be part of such a sweet memory for them.

I would stay in the colony until very early Monday morning, when I would get up and drive into Brooklyn to be at work by six o'clock.

While my family was away for the summer, my evenings were spent preparing the apartment with fresh paint and minor repairs for their homecoming and the Jewish holidays that would follow soon thereafter. Some evenings I spent time with my wife Mary's family or fellow survivors. Some of them I had met for the first time in the bungalow colony. We would get together at the pool, cooking out, or playing cards. Joe and Bernie Pearl were among these survivors and I would eventually find new employment with them.

In 1953, soon after moving to New York, I found Max Tepper, who had been my good friend, classmate, and teacher in Recklinghausen. He had also helped me prepare for my Bar Mitzvah in 1941. I also met people I had known in the Riga ghetto and Deggendorf DP Camp. We were a good support for one another, having shared a similar past, and we could exchange news about other people we had known who had survived. Our discussions included the restitution that was being offered by Germany for irreparable damage to our health, loss of parents, property, and education. We recalled memories of horrifying close calls and of the people who had not survived. We would meet at one another's homes, and I continue to stay in touch with those who are still alive to this day. We would often bring our spouses and children, to some of those meetings, and this is how our families bonded as well.

One of the other things that I determined at this point in my life was that most Holocaust survivors are not proud that we survived. We all feel a great deal of guilt for having done so, or for not doing more for those who did not. I know that I wish I could have done more for my mother and father even though I was only a kid when they each died.

Most survivors my age are not well educated, and as we emigrated to either America or other countries, we had to "fake" having the requisite education. Sometimes we would lie about our age so as to make our age and potential education more consistent with one another.

We also didn't talk about our experiences to outsiders, even to our families. Mary had no real interest in knowing of my experiences and I had no great need to share them with her. All she needed to know was that I was a survivor. In any event, I tried to bury as much of it as I could, and as deeply as I could. The only time you did talk about it was privately with other survivors. People did not want to know what we had gone through. In this case, ignorance was bliss for them.

Survivors who had tattooed numbers on their arms would hide them, fearing that people, seeing the number, would discriminate against them. It was known that younger survivors had very little, if any education, and the older ones carried a burden of fear and anger, all of which made employers hesitant to hire them. Many had not yet adapted to being free, and questioned why or if they should have survived. In many cases this feeling has never left them. It was also clear to all of us that we were often not respected by those that we encountered.

As I look back, I recall my first ten years in New York City with satisfaction. It was a good life, not great, but certainly adequate. We ate well, the boys gave me many reasons to be proud of them, and I was steadily advancing at my work in the retail grocery and kosher meat business. My efforts were recognized several times, and soon I found myself in a position to acquire an ownership interest in a business. This opportunity soon led to another. I was feeling better about myself with each passing year, though I knew in my heart of hearts that there were demons I had not dealt with, and it was probably only a matter of time before I would have to do so or suffer a great consequence.

This series of successful partnerships eventually allowed me to open my own business. I felt like a kid again. Free to be creative and to do what I thought was right. I closed the store and contracted to have it gutted and completely remodeled, refurnished, with new, modern self-service meat display cases and all the equipment necessary to operate a successful business.

Soon I was able to acquire a second business, and I worked night and day, sometimes sleeping in the stores, especially during the holidays. This was my routine for several years as I was completely immersed in my work. With two stores doing well, I was extremely busy. I had good help and always treated them well. I was motivated to do this because of the way I still felt inside about those who had mistreated me. By always going the extra mile, and being more generous than I needed to be, my staff quickly learned of my sincerity and willingness to give them the shirt off my back. They repaid me in loyalty and through their own forms of kindness. Had I to do it again, I would not change a thing in that regard.

Despite my professional success, the emotional scars that I carried continued to fester and eventually they began to drain me so much that at times I could not even work. I went into a depression. Given all of my other anger issues stemming from the Holocaust, I finally determined that it was time to seek professional help, which I did. I went to Long Island Jewish Hospital as an outpatient and was encouraged to join group therapy. This was merely the first step on a long road to recovery. I also know that I would not be the person I am today without having admitting to myself that I needed help. I am grateful to the doctors who so ably treated me.

With my children long since grown, my business affairs in order, I realized that maybe it was time to consider what the next phase of my life would be. I had visited in Florida for several winters. My sister, Alice and her daughter, Jeannette, lived there. Also, a number of my friends had retired there, and I contemplated a return to Florida to settle there permanently. While I was deciding what to do, I went to Richmond, Virginia to visit my niece, Esther Binshtok and her husband, Meir for his birthday in August, 1994. Meir convinced me that I probably would not be happy in Florida or I would have bought a place there over the past years.

With Florida off of the list, I decided to come full circle and relocate to Richmond. Not being quite ready to retire, I worked with my nephew for a few years, and finally stopped working in 1999 at the age of 72. I was content with the idea that I would spend my last years in blissful retirement. I should have known better, and that Fate would intervene.

29. Welcome sign greeting Alex at the Haltern Realschule.

30. Placard sign for Schule Ohne Rassismus, Schule Mit Courage (School without Racism, School with Courage.) This is a national recognition bestowed on select schools throughout Germany that meet strict criterion. See Appendix A.

31. Cover of the book compiled by students at the Realschule that was later sold on the streets of Haltern at a cost of 10 DM. *1995 Haltern: Die Gesichte Der Juden im Haltern (The History of the Jews in Haltern).*

32. Newspaper ad promoting the Realschule's activities and Alex's support of the projects with his presence in Haltern.

33. Alex speaking at Ort gegen das Vergessen (The Place of No Return) commemorating the departing Jews from the City of Haltern.

34. Ort gegen das Vergessen – Place of No Return.

35. Exterior of the 1908 vintage cattle car acquired and refurbished by the students at the Realschule as a lasting memorial to all those who perished during the persecution of the Jews.

36. When the railroad car was relocated from a station siding to the grounds of the Realschule the work was done by the Mertmann Company completely free of charge. Principal Michael Weiand (center) honors the company for their generosity.

37. Inside the cattle car: a display that depicts Jewish life before, during, and after Hitler. Note the side by side pictures of Natan and Lotte Lebenstein previously depicted in this book.

ZUM ANDENKEN AN UNSERE JÜDISCHEN
BÜRGERINNEN UND BÜRGER, DIE IN
DEN JAHREN 1933–1945
GEDEMÜTIGT, ENTRECHTET, VERTRIEBEN
UND ERMORDET WURDEN.

לזכר עולם

VERSTORBEN IN AUSCHWITZ
DANIEL HEINRICH ✳ 1888
FRESCO FANNY ✳ 1879
MEYER JAKOB ✳ 1886
MEYER ROSALIE GEB.HERTZ
PINS SARA GEB.MEYER ✳ 1870

VERSCHOLLEN IN AUSCHWITZ
DANIEL ELLA GEB.HAYUM ✳ 1894
DANIEL HANNELORE ✳ 1928
HAMACHER KARL ✳ 1902
LEBENSTEIN CHARLOTTE GEB.JOSEPHS ✳ 1884

VERSTORBEN IN CHOLM
HERZFELD ROSALIE GEB.ELSER ✳ 1881

VERSCHOLLEN IN MINSK
COHEN LEONHARD ✳ 1866
WEYL ABRAHAM ✳ 1869

VERSTORBEN IN RIGA
LEBENSTEIN NATHAN ✳ 1880

VERSCHOLLEN IN RIGA
HERZFELD FRITZ-OTTO ✳ 1911
KLEEBERG JEANETTE GEB.GOTTSCHALK ✳ 1885

VERSTORBEN IN THERESIENSTADT
LEBENSTEIN RANETTE ✳ 1867
ROSENBERG ANNA ✳ 1867

UNBEKANNT VERSTORBEN
COHN HERMANN ✳ 1873
MEYER MAX ✳ 1888

UNBEKANNT VERSCHOLLEN
MEYER CAECILIA ✳ 1877
MEYER CORA ✳ 1874
MEYER JETTE ✳ 1878

תנצבה

„IHR ALLE, DIE IHR VORÜBERGEHT,
KOMMT UND SEHT, OB
EIN SCHMERZ SEI WIE EIN SCHMERZ
DER MAN MIR ANGETAN"

38. The cemetery marker purchased by the students of the Realschule with proceeds of the book *Die Gesichte Der Juden im Haltern*. The acknowledgment that Alex survived is unfortunately lost in the grass.

166

39. Students marching in commemoration of *Kristallnacht*

40. Students marching in commemoration of *Kristallnacht*.
Burgermeister Erwin Kirschenbaum is in the foreground with his
camera.

41. Up close and personal with Alex.

42. Alex being swarmed by his adoring children

43. Teaching from his large book of articles, pictures, and other memorabilia at Virginia Commonwealth University in Richmond, VA.

44. Alex with sons David and Danny at Shea Stadium in New York.

45. A triumphant Alex leaving the opening of the cattle car memorial
on the grounds of the Realschule. He is reacting to the following
picture.

46. The children of the Realschule express their feelings for godfather
Alex.

47. The superstar-laden soccer team of Schalke 04 protests against racism.

48. The Star of David figures prominently in another commemoration of Kristallnacht conducted by the students of the Realschule.

49. Alex and 91-year old Frau Plum (nee Sondermann) owner and operator of the Hotel in which Alex and his family sought refuge on the night of November 10, 1938.

50. Alex with Erwin and Tina Kirschenbaum in Richmond, VA on one of their visits to the United States.

51. Stolpersteine that introduces the project as a remembrance to those who lived through or perished in the horrors of 1933-1945.

52. The *Stolpersteine* (stumbling stones) being added to the sidewalks and streets of Haltern by Gunter Demnig.

53. The three stones commemorating Natan, Lotte, and Alex
    Lebenstein in front of Disselhof 36.

54. Alex examining the stones in front of Disselhof 36 on one of his
    visits.

55. Thomas Schwieren, the owner of the newly constructed Disselhof 36 and the commemorate plaque that honors the Lebenstein family.

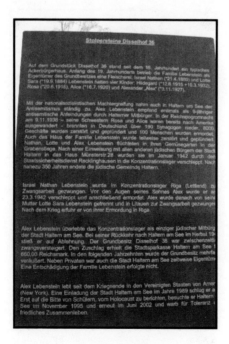

56. The plaque that can be seen by pedestrians as they pass the new Disselhof 36.

57. Planting Alex's apple tree on the grounds of the Realschule.

58. Alex's apple tree will someday provide shade for the memorial to those who perished during the Holocaust.

59. Tears of Isieu being formed in front of the cattle car by collecting the drops of melting ice.

60. Stones with the names representing each of the 44 French children from the town of Isieu who were murdered by the Nazis in 1944.

61. The Virginia Holocaust Museum receives its own cattle car.

62. Elie Wiesel and Eliese Levin, one of Alex's new children, during one of Dr. Wiesel's visits to Richmond, VA.

63. Alex and Elie Wiesel

64. Alex celebrates his 80th birthday on November 3, 2007.

65. Memorial at Riga –Bikernieki with ancillary stones that have
    names of known and presumed victims of the mass killings that
    took place in 1941-1942.

66. Alex with Georg and Erica Nockemann in Haltern.

67. Alex and war-time friend Ewald Aul holding pictures of themselves taken at the end of the war in 1945.

68. Burgermeister Bodo Klimpel at the time of the Ehrenburger
ceremonies.

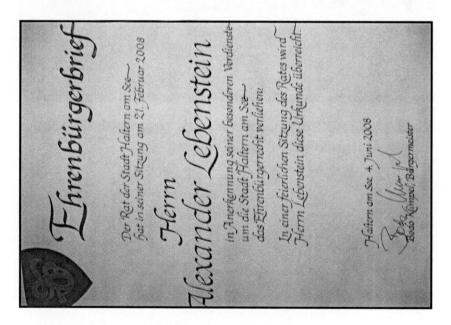

69. The Ehrenburger certificate.

70. Alex holds the Ehrenburger (honored citizen) declaration filled
    with the signatures of all the city elders.

71. Alex and Realschule Principal Michael Weiand.

72. The Alexander-Lebenstein-Realschule of Haltern am See is unveiled.

73. Alex Lebenstein and Don Levin, celebrating the completion of the editing process.

PART IV

Tolerance

Chapter 21

Passages

"And kill all the dogs too."

In the late 1970s, Alex's older son, David, made an introduction over lunch between his father and a gentleman that he knew had shared similar experiences during the war. So it was that Alex and Ernie Haas became acquainted, and formed a friendship that continues to this day as both men enjoy life as octogenarians. A few years older than Alex, Ernie had also immigrated to the United States after the war and settled in Montclaire, New Jersey.

Unlike Alex, Ernie had retained his roots to his German culture. Being older, he had a higher education. He had been in the Riga Ghetto when Alex and his parents were there and also in the concentration camps at Kaiserwald and Burggrabben. While they had not known one another, they shared the common horrors of those times and places.

Over the years, in an effort to maintain the cultural ties to his native land, Ernie faithfully read the German newspaper, Aufbau. In 1988, he discovered an advertisement by the International Red Cross, for the city of Haltern, seeking the whereabouts of one Alexander Lebenstein.

When Ernie read this, he immediately called Alex and encouraged him to contact the city. After numerous adamant refusals, Alex finally relented and told Ernie that he could contact Haltern, so long as he did not reveal to them where Alex was currently residing. With this passive consent, Ernie contacted the City of Haltern. For the next few years there was a regular exchange of correspondence between Ernie and Haltern on Alex's behalf. Each letter contained an invitation, wanting this former citizen, the sole Jewish survivor from Haltern who survived the concentration camps, to come for a visit at the City's expense. Alex refused every offer and Ernie would respond with excuses for him.

The fires of hatred that had burned so intensely for fifty plus years had not diminished with the passage of time. The anger and frustration that Alex had bottled up inside of him more resembled smoldering embers waiting to burst into flame when exposed to a fresh source of oxygen. The tinder to ignite this blaze was the mere idea of his returning to Germany under any circumstances. The mere suggestion was enough to send him into a rage.

It was in 1994 that Alex received two handwritten letters from students who were growing up and attending school in the city of Haltern. A change in policy now permitted them to study about the Holocaust and to have access to the detailed records carefully compiled and chronicled in the City Archives. Questions posed to older family members left them with even more questions. Finally, two of them mustered the courage to write to Alex, and Alex's resolve to never set foot in Germany again began to melt.

There are certain experiences that are beyond description and comprehension, and unless you have lived them, you cannot possibly relate to them. Finding Ernie the way I did gave me an outlet, another avenue of support, and more importantly, a friend in whom I could confide. Ernie is also a person whom I greatly respect. I did not realize how important our friendship would be until 1988 when Ernie contacted me about something that he had read in a German newspaper urging me to contact the City of Haltern am See.

"Look Ernie, I don't speak German, I don't write it, and I don't even think it any more. Why should I contact them?"

"Maybe they have some property or something that belongs to you," he joked.

"They can go to hell. I don't want anything from them."

"But Alex, maybe they have something that rightfully belongs to you," Ernie argued. "That sort of thing is happening every day now."

"Let them keep it all. I don't want it."

"Alex, maybe they want to somehow make amends. You have nothing to lose by letting them know where you live," he implored.

"Ernie, you know I don't write German anymore. Anyway, it doesn't matter. I want nothing to do with any of them. I am an American now, and that chapter of my life is closed!"

"Listen, Alex, I'll be glad to write a letter for you."

"If you want to do that for me, I would accept. But don't let them know where I live."

I was shocked by the audacity and insensitivity of this city when one of the invitations asked me to attend the celebration of the 750th anniversary of the founding of this Roman Catholic town. For me, it added insult to injury as my memory went back to the time when vile anti-Semitism was preached from the pulpits of the Roman Catholic churches. As a result, untold hurt, destruction and death were inflicted on the Jewish population of this city and elsewhere.

As I imagined my possible return to Germany, I experienced a flashback and recalled an event I had witnessed in my childhood. *Schutzenfest* was a time when a king and queen were crowned and set upon a hay wagon, drawn by a single horse. The *Oompah* band accompanied this procession, and people all over applauded. In my mind I thought, "What will they do with me if I go there? Will they celebrate the 750th anniversary of the city's founding by placing the sole surviving Jew from this city on a hay wagon? Would the Nazi groups that are still all around, even in this city, try to take advantage and kill the only surviving Jew?" My imagination went wild, and I thought, "Let them drop dead!" My pain and anger quickly threatened to consume me. I swore I would never return to that city. And I asked Ernie to let them know not to write to me again.

I hated the people, the children, and even the dogs. I really did want to kill the dogs – the German Shepherds – who were always there to nip at our heels if we did not move fast enough, or in the direction that we had been instructed to march. I realized that I was still messed up. I knew it but did not know what to do about it.

And then, like a miracle, a bridge of peace and love began to fall into place. That this would ever happen to me is an unexpected blessing from God.

It was 1994, and I received two handwritten letters from students within the town of Haltern. When I first received those letters my first impression was, "How dare they invite me again, now using students as a decoy." I felt that it was asking quite a lot of me to return to Germany and dredge up all of these horrible memories I had been forced to live with all of these fifty plus years. I did not want to ever set foot on the bloody cobblestones of Germany again. I knew that there were still Nazis alive who would probably get a thrill out of killing an old Jew, especially if he was the only survivor of the camps from the town. That was one of the crazy thoughts that went through my mind.

What made my position especially difficult was when my family started to say things like, "You are the most intolerant person we know. You ask us not to be prejudiced, and yet there you sit telling us about how you would kill every last German if you had the chance. You cannot deny these young people the opportunity to hear the truth from a Holocaust survivor. Shame on you for being so selfish and not helping these children."

Well, as far as I was concerned, no matter what the officials were asking of me or what these letters said, they were all written by the children and grandchildren of Nazis and I wanted nothing to do with them. At that point in time, if I had access to a bomb, I would have used it to kill them. I remained resolved to resisting the pressure of my friends and family, and never to go back to Haltern under any circumstances.

Then my family and friends began to talk to me even more directly, and they would say, "You have to go! You have to go back to Germany for the sake of the children," or "You must do this. It is the only way that you can set things straight in your own heart, and insure that they learn the Truth that you keep telling us is so important for the world to know."

I finally gave in to the pressure that was being put on me and accepted the student's invitation to visit their school. We scheduled the trip for November of 1995. It was agreed that my niece, Esther Binshtok, would travel with me as my companion and to provide moral support. It was also important for her to learn about her mother's roots in Haltern as well as her father's roots in Enger, a town located not too far from Haltern. All of the travel arrangements were made for us by the City of Haltern, and we received a large packet containing our itineraries. While we definitely began to feel a little bit like celebrities, I also felt a great foreboding falling over me. I was very nervous on the flight, as over and over again I questioned myself about whether this was the right thing for me to be doing.

I remember when we arrived at the airport in Dusseldorf and my feet first touched German soil again. With each step I thought about the Allied soldiers who had given their lives to rid this land of the tyranny of Hitler. I thought of the countless innocents, to include my parents, who had died when the ground ran red with blood. Yet, here I was again on this blood soaked ground. It was both painful and frightening, as I felt myself begin to sweat and to feel overwhelmed by a great feeling of foreboding.

We were met by Georg Nockemann, the City spokesperson. I knew who he was from a picture of him that had been sent to me. He was there to greet us on behalf of the *Burgermeister* (Mayor), Erwin Kirschenbaum. My first reaction at seeing him through the window, waving to us as if he were greeting a long lost friend or relative, was that he or his family might have a Nazi past. I have since come to know him and his wife, Erica, as wonderful people, and I am privileged to count them among my friends. He was standing there with a big grin on his face, very sincere in his desire to make us feel welcome. I am ashamed to say that my initial reactions were prompted by my own prejudices and insecurities. I was under protest from within myself.

Our one hour ground transportation back to Haltern am See was uneventful but extremely uncomfortable. As I sat watching the countryside go whizzing by outside the window, I was struck by the fact that all the bombed-out buildings and evidence of death and destruction from the war were gone. This was in stark contrast to my last memories of Germany some fifty years ago. Despite this change, I still found myself very ill at ease.

I was not completely oblivious and self-absorbed. I recall that the ride was as uncomfortable for Georg as it was for me, albeit for different reasons. He was trying to tell me about the daily itineraries which he had very methodically assembled and I of course did not want to hear any of it. I just wanted to be left alone. Georg was attempting his best to speak to me in both German and broken English, whereas I was not cutting him any slack, and would only speak English to him.

It was already late in the afternoon when we arrived in what had once been my hometown. It was hard to comprehend that this was the place where I was born, and where my family had once lived. At first, there was very little I recognized; so much had changed.

We went directly to the Hotel Sondermann. It was truly bittersweet for me to return to the very hotel in which we were hidden after that terrible night in the cemetery during *Kristallnacht*, from November 10 to 11, 1938. The rooms that they had reserved for us were very lovely and a wave of nostalgia overwhelmed me as I remembered our time in the basement, as well as the kindness that had been extended to us during that horrible time. The next day I was able to introduce Esther to Anne Plum, still the hotel owner, who was now 83 years old. She had taken such a risk when she provided us shelter in her basement in 1938.

The first evening, after a short rest, we were taken out to dinner to meet the Mayor, Erwin Kirschenbaum, and other city officials. Everyone was doing their level best to make us feel welcome, and I remember finding it strange to accept their kindness. After the festivities had ended, it was a long and lonely night for me even though my niece was in the next room. I don't know if it was jetlag, nerves, or merely anticipation of what lay ahead. Emotions and memories overwhelmed me, and sleep would not come as the ghosts of the past haunted my mind.

All of that changed the next day when I finally met the children. The children. Always the children.

Esther and I were picked up at the hotel by Georg Nockemann and several students and we quickly walked over to the school. Haltern remains a compact little town, and after a five block walk we arrived at the Hermann Boeckler Trade School. We were taken on a tour and introduced informally to the principal, the teachers, and a few other members of the community who had gathered. It was then explained to me again that I would be able to speak to any number of students in the course of my visit. Looking back, I must say that I was overwhelmed simply by my experiences in talking to individual students, much less to those gathered in the assembly hall. At this point my skills at speaking

German were marginal at best, so I was speaking through an interpreter, Erica Nockemann, Georg's wife, who is an English teacher. In addition to my prepared remarks, we also allowed time for several question and answer sessions, which were physically and emotionally draining for me.

Adding to the raw anxiety of the week-long visit was of course the fact that this was also the week for the commemoration of *Kristallnacht*. I found this to be an incredibly emotional experience for myself. I was very grateful that my niece Esther was there to give me strength and reassurance.

The next day, two young ladies approached me, and I recognized that they were just as frightened of me as I was of them. I was astounded when one of them finally asked me in English, "Mr. Lebenstein, may I hold your hand?"

"You want to hold my hand? Why would you want to do that," I asked. "I am not holy."

"To me you are," she said, and then I knew that the tears both girls were shedding did not come from their eyes, but rather from their hearts.

The other asked, "Can you forgive me?"

"Forgive you for what? You have done nothing wrong to me."

"We feel so much pain and shame for what happened to you and your family, and the Jewish people," she cried, obviously in a great deal of distress.

"But you were not even alive then. When was your mother born?" I asked in an effort to make my point clear to them.

"1949," was the near-whisper response.

"Well, even she was not born then," I assured her.

"It is very degrading for us to discover how you and your people were mistreated by our grandparents. It is something for which we have to shoulder some responsibility too."

"No," I said. "It is your grandfather who is guilty. Not you. He would not have the courage or the decency, to ask me for forgiveness, would he? And I would not forgive him. But you have done nothing for which you have to ask my forgiveness."

"I have asked my grandfather what happened during the war, and he tells me that nothing of the sort happened. That everything we are learning about now is nothing more than fiction, and the Holocaust is a creation of the United States, Great Britain, and the Jews."

"It happened. I am living proof of that. This kind of denial is typical of people your grandfather's age." I said firmly, attempting to reassure her.

"I know that. I have read what is in the archives. But when I challenge him now and say 'Grandfather, you always loved me and taught me to tell the truth. When I was little, you bounced me on your knee and sang songs to me. Now, I want you to tell me the truth,' and all I am greeted with is his silence, for he has no more words to give to me," she said quietly.

I was stunned when I saw the pain these students were living with. They were confronting the truth of the horror wrought by their grandparents and in some cases parents. I explained to them that there was never going to be a time that I could forgive the Nazis for the despicable things they did to me, my parents, and the world at large. But, in an effort to offer some consolation, I let them know that those who served in the German Army, were soldiers doing their duty for their country, and unlike the SS, certainly not all were Nazis. I am not certain how much solace they were able to take in these words, but at that moment, I felt something deep inside of me when I realized just how much these children were suffering because of what their forefathers had done fifty and sixty years ago. My advice was, rather than to carry guilt and pain, they should turn their energies into teaching tolerance.

It was also on this first trip back to Germany that some of the old feelings I had feared would return came roaring back at me. I was in my hotel room, just getting dressed early in the morning to go and to have a meeting with the kids at the school, when it happened. I had already been there two or three days. While I was definitely more at ease, something kept me from being totally relaxed and comfortable. The anger had begun to leave me because of the budding connections I had made with youngsters at the several schools we visited.

I saw their pain and suffering as they learned the truth, and my sympathy for them was starting to grow. I was also surprised by the sincere love and admiration coming from the children, as well as from people who remembered me from my childhood and came to see me.

So, I was in my room dressing, when all of a sudden there was a knock at my door. I opened the door and found the smiling face of Monica Plum, the daughter-in-law of the woman who had hidden us so many years ago. She was now managing the hotel and had come to inquire if I would be coming to the breakfast room, a small sitting room off the lobby. I told her that I still needed a few minutes. She then informed me that a man was waiting who wanted to say hello. Her exact words were, "He wants to have an 'audience' with you." I asked her to tell my mystery guest that I would be there shortly.

When I walked into the foyer, I was told my guest was waiting for me in the breakfast room. As I entered, I found this man standing erect, arms crossed over his chest, in an arrogant, Nazi-like position. Nonetheless, I greeted him with a smile on my face, and asked, "Good morning. Sorry I kept you waiting. What can I do for you?"

He replied, "You don't remember me?"

I asked, "Am I supposed to?"

He said, "You should! How could you forget me?"

Starting to feel apprehensive, I asked, "Why am I supposed to remember you? It has been fifty years since I left Haltern."

"You should remember me, you know."

"Okay, so tell me why?" I asked, trying to manage a smile.

Then he retorted furiously, "We went to kindergarten and the first three grades together. When we had our Catholic lesson, you were excused and went home. Remember when we always chipped in money and gave it to you so that after our lesson, at recess, you would bring back a *Beenenstich* (beehive cake -- sweet cake with almonds)? You always brought it back, and I remember you ate from it, but never put in any of your money to buy it."

I was at a loss for words; I didn't know if I should laugh in his face or to toss him out on his ear. He was so serious about it.

Then he continued, "But you should know me! Don't you remember when you came back from the concentration camp and I met you in the marketplace, wearing my uniform. I wore it so proudly, and you tore it off of me!" he shouted angrily.

My memories of that time came back, and my whole face changed as anger built inside me. "Now, I remember! I don't remember you, but I recall ripping off a Nazi uniform jacket from somebody in the marketplace!" And grinning, I asked, "That was you?"

"I will never forgive you for what you did to me that day and for not chipping in for the *Beenenstich* either," he replied.

"Get the hell out of here, or I'll tear you apart again," I roared. And he left without saying another word.

Some years later, in 2003, when I was once again in Haltern, I was seated at an outdoor café in the market place with my son, David, and grandson, Adam. Whom did I see sitting at a nearby table? It was the same man. This time I just stared him down. He simply grinned back at me and sort of raised his glass as if in salute to me. I guess he had seen that I had made a difference in Haltern by doing good things with the students.

There was one more disturbing incident on this first visit. The students had obtained permission to hang a Nazi flag as part of an exhibit portraying life for the Jews in Haltern, before, during, and after the Third Reich. The exhibit was set up inside the old city hall, and the flag hung near a window, visible from the street. Halfway during the presentation, a number of "skin heads" entered the City Hall hoping to join what they thought was a Nazi rally in progress. This was further evidence that the Nazi culture was still alive and well within Haltern and probably throughout all of Germany.

In hindsight, after these negative experiences, I know that, were it not for the wonderful students and their supportive faculties, I would never have gone back to Germany. They did more for me during that first trip than I could ever have imagined doing for them.

At the end of the week, I was the subject of a number of newspaper interviews. The reporter wanted to know, "How did it go for you?" My answers were very blunt; I did not hold back anything. I told him that none of the city's past invitations were meaningful enough for me to compromise myself. I had been especially insulted by the one in 1989 when the city of Haltern wanted me to come to help celebrate the 750th anniversary of the city that had done me so much harm. I also let the reporter know that, without the touching letters from the students asking for help, I would never have come at all. Had it not been for the letters, the urging of my family, and my niece's willingness to accompany me, we would not be sitting there together sharing an interview.

While we were quite overjoyed at the reception we received from the students as well as the townspeople, I still had very conflicted emotions when it came time for us to return to the United States. While I had resolved to help those fine young German people overcome their pain and I had agreed to work with the school and to be an example of tolerance, I was still unsure of my commitment and whether I could live up to it.

As we flew home, I remember wondering if I could learn to practice what I was preaching and in turn become more tolerant. I realized that I was still harboring angry feelings about the horrible past and the shocking incidents that had occurred during my visit. How could I possibly change my ways and teach tolerance?

While it truly was the partial closure of an ugly door and the opening of a beautiful window that probably saved my life, I felt extremely torn. You just don't dump fifty years of pent-up anger and frustration overnight. No doubt about it, the students had gotten to me. They reached inside of me to places that I had not gone in over fifty years. Once we were back in Richmond, I began to reach out for help to ease my pain. Little did I know just how much my life would continue to evolve as I, too, began my own transformation.

Shortly after I left for home, the children pooled their efforts and put together a book about the exhibit in the Haltern City Hall that depicted Jewish life before, during, and after Hitler. It also included recent news clippings and described the impact of my return on them and to the city. They sold the book in the marketplace before Christmas for ten *Deutsch Mark* and raised quite a bit of money. They then petitioned the city council for permission to use these funds to erect a memorial to all the Jews of Haltern who perished during the Holocaust. My parents are listed on this memorial as well, which stands on a corner of what was left of the old Jewish cemetery after the destruction on *Kristallnacht*.

I am often asked whether it bothers me that my parents don't have a grave stone, and I don't know what really happened to my mother. My father's fate was clear cut; nobody had to describe to me the when or how he was taken from us. He was buried inside the Riga ghetto. Because of the cold, the mass graves were left open all winter. It was so cold that the bodies were frozen. No funerals or memorials were allowed for any of these people. The bodies would stay there open until the grave was full and only then would they cover it all up. Both of my parents are memorialized on the marker in Haltern. I consoled myself with the knowledge that my father and mother are with all the other fathers and mothers who endured the same atrocities and perished together. The monuments that are there in Riga today indicate they honor all those people who died from 1938 – 1944.

I am frequently asked when it was that I finally gave up hope of seeing my mother alive and well. Truthfully, I did not give up hope of my mother being alive until well after the war was over, and even after she was not in Haltern to meet me. Once I was in the DP camp, I would hear reunions that often began, "Oh I thought you were dead," and I would again be filled with some measure of hope that my mother could still be alive. Perhaps she was injured or too frail, and maybe I would stumble over her some day soon. After all, the only thing that I had been told when I returned from the peat bogs to the ghetto in Riga was she had been transferred to another camp for work. I wanted to believe that so badly I just made it my reality. Of course when I learned that nobody like my mother, a woman without a husband, not in the absolute best shape to work, ever was transferred to another camp unless it was to a death camp such as Auschwitz or Birkenau, then I lost hope of her survival, and started to believe that she was probably buried either in the ghetto or outside it in the forest in another mass grave. For these reasons, I paid for my parents' names to be entered on a grave stone in Bikernieki outside of Riga, Latvia so that they will always be remembered there as well.

I know that because of my work with the children of Haltern I am a much different person than I was prior to going. I don't know if I would even be alive had I not made that first trip. Truly it was a new lease on life. I am a much nicer person today than I was in 1995.

I also realize that if I had related my wartime experiences to anyone prior to going back to visit with the children in 1995, my perspective and accounts would be totally different as well, largely because I didn't think anyone would believe me -- the stories were just so horrible to tell. People who did not live through it can't relate, and those who did experience it certainly did not want to relive it. I don't recall any special feelings on Mary's part towards me simply because I was a survivor. It was just an accepted state of being: I was a survivor. I may not have had a number tattooed on my arm as a daily reminder, but I was a survivor nonetheless. I guess the other major difference is that I am more at peace with myself. I have not forgiven the Nazis or the Germans of that generation for any of the crimes and injustices they wrought on me, my family, and the world at large, but at least now I am not letting it eat me up.

Looking back, I realize that I had compartmentalized almost all of my teenaged years in a deep dark corner of my mind. By ignoring it, I did myself, my children, and a good number of people around me a great disservice. In fairness however, I don't know if I would have been able to survive at all had I not done this like so many other survivors also did. The horrific images of death that had been tattooed in my heart and soul can never be forgotten, but to dwell on them every day would mean certain insanity for me. It was also the only way that I could manage to keep this deep-seated anger in check.

I tell all of my "new" children that I spent the better part of fifty years angry with the world around me because there were certain aspects of the experience that I could not suppress. It was an anger that should have consumed me long ago. Yet, it did not, and for some reason, God spared me. I will never forget it and use it, as a teaching tool when I am with the children.

Of course over the years there were also visual reminders that would trigger these horrible memories. One very powerful one, to this day, is policemen patrolling on horseback or on motorcycles, wearing tall leather boots. I look at those boots and feel a bad energy force go through my body. I experience the full range of emotions: fear, anger, and anxiety, until I calm myself down.

When I returned to Richmond from my first trip to Haltern, I was very angry with myself. I was angry that I had gone at all and allowed myself to relive the horrors of *Kristallnacht* and all of the years that followed.

I was angry to discover that the government had built a highway over two thirds of the Jewish cemetery and that a concrete road now rests over the graves of my grandparents. I was feeling all of the hurt again. I was questioning whether I was sincere about wanting to work with the children over there and teaching them about what was in the archives, and the whole idea of teaching them about tolerance. But the resolve to do just this certainly grew after I reflected on it, and received reassurance from other people around me. I must candidly admit that it was also the first time that I really addressed a great number of the issues that had bothered me all of my life, and I sought out professional help again. Counseling was a wonderful gift to myself, providing discovery, growth, and healing.

You don't have to live in the past to respect it. We are in the present, but must learn from the past in order to teach lessons from it, so that the future is not a repeat of the past.

CHAPTER 22

Angel on my Shoulder: Mission in Life

"I did not know what to do with my feelings."

I was down and out after visiting the kids in Germany. My heart and soul were in a constant state of torment, as I tried to determine what my future, if any, should be in terms of reaching out to this new generation. No doubt about it, the kids had certainly gotten under my skin in ways I could never have imagined. I hated them, I didn't hate them. I cared, I didn't care. I didn't know what to feel. The trip had certainly thrown me for a real loop. By the time that I returned to Richmond, I was in very bad shape. All at the same time I felt betrayed and lost, yet focused, energized, and maybe even redeemed.

It raised other issues for me as well – personal ones. For I realized that now I was in a position of sharing all of my experiences with perfect strangers; and yet, after all of these years, I had still not shared these same life altering experiences with any of my family. My boys largely still did not know about the horrors that I, their grandparents, and millions like us, all had endured. It is their birthright, and yet they didn't know it. When they were young, and I would meet with other survivors in New York City, the kids would play with one another oblivious to the conversation of the adults as we sat and visited. Clearly, the preparation for and aftermath of my trip back to Haltern was the most exposure they had ever received, and I suspect that in their minds it was largely just an account of my travels and current experiences. It did not include any of the real germane pieces of history.

It was also during this time that I came to the realization that anyone, including me, who ever achieves anything remotely great, does not accomplish it on their own; to think otherwise is simply nonsense. More often than not, they have an angel sitting on their shoulder. My angel has a name, and her name is Miriam Davidow.

At that time, Miriam was the Director of Community Relations at the Jewish Community Federation of Richmond, and she oversaw all the Holocaust memorial events, and would coordinate requests for survivors to come and speak to various groups. She would receive requests from schools, civic groups, Army bases, churches, and just about any group that had an interest in the Holocaust in general. She is well known, greatly respected, and very influential in the community and in the political realm. I am proud to count her among my friends. She truly became an angel on my shoulder. I have known her family for a number of years now, and don't know where I would be without her.

From the time that I met her, Miriam was always encouraging me to share my story. While she had several other survivors whom she would ask to fill these speaking engagements, once she heard of my story, and realized how much I was hurting inside, she took it upon herself to draw me into her circle, and get me to participate in these engagements. She helped me overcome the pain, the confusion, and extreme anger that, at times, almost paralyzed me. I kept having the image of those kids I had met coming back to me in my mind. I almost felt like they were touching me. I could not help myself because I was so torn. The harshest reality was that at the time I had pledged support to these young kids whose mothers had not even been born at the time of the war, I really did not mean it the way it sounded. I said it to be nice, and to comfort them, without any real intent of doing anything beyond uttering those words. But that kept coming back to me over and over. It bothered me that I did not really feel any form of commitment when I had said it, and so I would get down on myself for this too. There were all these negative feelings to deal with burbling up from deep within my soul.

I can still hear Miriam saying, "Alex you cannot keep this inside of you. You have to talk about it and get it out of your system. I have a good idea. You have to talk to people in schools about your experiences."

"Come on Miriam, you know very well that I am not a public speaker."

"You can do it, Alex, I know you can. I also know that you must do it! Trust me this will also help you to sort out your feelings."

A few days later, Miriam called me and said she had a place she wanted me to speak, and that she would go with me. I told her that if she was serious about going with me, I would agree to do the talk. Needless to say I was extremely nervous that first time, but Miriam was there to support and encourage me.

My first talk was to a group of interested Army Reserve soldiers in late 1996 or early 1997. It was supposed to be a forty-five minute talk. Even when a general came in and wanted to break for lunch, everyone stayed in place for another forty-five minutes. It was incredible to me that people were so eager to hear my story. This first talk gave me the confidence that Miriam had promised. The amazing thing was how free I felt, and how easy it became to answer some of the painful questions they posed.

Miriam had been right; the key to my living a more normal life was to purge some of the anger and hate from my system by talking about it. It was very much like ripping off the scabs so many years ago to rid myself of the lice that were making me so sick; so it was that I needed to rip off the emotional scabs. Of course now, years later, I sometimes physically act out a good bit of my story because I have become so comfortable with public speaking.

It has become a win-win situation for everyone - for me, the students in Haltern, and now, for those who learn from my presentations throughout the greater Richmond metropolitan area. It is gratifying to me to know that all of us, regardless of age, color, race, creed, are able to change for the better.

At the same time my contacts with Germany were beginning, and the work in Virginia was exploding, another angel appeared - my old friend Inge Windmueller, now married to Harold Horowitz. I had first met Inge when I came to Virginia in 1947, at events sponsored by the New American Jewish Club. I did not see her for nearly fifty years after that, as I went to Florida and she entered college. We became reacquainted when I returned for my sister Rose's funeral in the early 1990s. When I relocated to Richmond in 1995, Inge and I met again. She was active on the Holocaust Education Committee and was the person who introduced me to Miriam Davidow.

Inge accompanied me on many of my early speaking engagements to provide support. I shared with her my growing correspondence from Germany and from students in the local schools, and she realized that I needed help. I did not have a computer nor was I able to answer letters adequately in English. She did so much for me in handling the huge volume of e-mail that came to her address. There were many requests from individuals and groups for my help on projects and book reports. Sometimes I needed to prepare a speech or an article for publication. Inge would assist me by both typing and editing my responses. She helped me organize my scribbles on yellow pads into coherent thoughts with the proper words and grammar.

As the speaking requests mushroomed, I decided to give up my job and working income to devote myself totally to what I now called "My Work." In addition to Miriam and Inge who were always willing to accompany me, soon my companion, Celeste Kocen, also began to do so as well. Now, as I am older and increasingly busier, my good friend Susie Levin willingly handles the bulk of the scheduling of my presentations and also accompanies me on these engagements, sometimes driving me if the distance is great, always ready to lend me support and encouragement. As we were gathering materials for this book, a good bit of the time Don and I were joined by Susie. I am very blessed to have such a great cheering section. Now I am very busy, and sometimes have to decline invitations to speak because of time, distance, or simply because at eighty one years of age, I don't have the physical stamina I once had. I am grateful for both the company and encouragement and the occasional chauffeuring, when I conduct these speaking engagements.

Chapter 23

A New Life

"For a very long time, life was a fight for existence. Now it is a fight for good."

In the course of many hours together, tracing the individual threads of the tapestry that has formed this incredible man's life, one must make the observation that but for the letters from the children of Haltern which so dramatically changed his life, the rage and hate that burned so hotly, probably would have consumed this man long ago. Much like the flames that licked at the pages of 20,000 books that were destroyed a mere 100 days after Adolf Hitler's legal rise to power on the night of May 10, 1933, so it was with the rage and hate that still threatened to consume Alex fifty years after the end of the war. It was the desire of both the children and Alex to reach out to one another that allowed a bridge of friendship and respect to be established. This bridge has spawned so many great works in the past thirteen years.

Visitors to the Virginia Holocaust Museum today are greeted by the sight of an original cattle car, vintage 1909, that has not been restored to the same degree as the one at the Haltern Realschule has been. The process by which it was obtained actually started on a dare from the Founder and Executive Director of the museum, Jay Ipson to Alex Lebenstein.

Alex mentioned to Jay that the kids over in Haltern acquired a cattle car for the memorial on the school grounds. He did not believe Alex. He did not believe it because he knew that they were in fact "scarcer than hen's teeth," and that he himself had looked and that there were none to be had. "I've been looking for years for one. It's like looking for a needle in a haystack."

So how does a man so full of rage and hate for over half a century become committed to easing the pain of a new generation of Germany? Simple. It is the children. With each passing group of children that attends the Realschule, the projects get bigger, more symbolic, and take on greater meaning.

It was on the October 2006 visit to Haltern upon exiting the cattle car memorial that Alex witnessed his children showing their feelings for him by forming a large heart on the plaza outside the cattle car.

When I was very young and learned "love thy neighbor as thyself," it meant the entire neighborhood of people who lived around me. Today the world has become our neighborhood, and love and tolerance must be shared with all mankind.

As I sit and watch the news on television from the comfort of my soft leather chair, which itself I don't take for granted, it pains me to see reports from Darfur and other places where there is injustice in the world. So much suffering and cruelty still exist today. The shocking reports that headline the news on television go right through me. My heart aches when I hear of intolerance. I will often suffer a flashback that can haunt my sleep that night.

No doubt about it, the transition to this phase of my life, began with the first trip to Haltern...and the children. Until then I really did not know why God had spared me or what I was supposed to do with the rest of my life. While I was generally healthy, had provided for my needs, and was looking forward to retirement, my life had taken on a new dimension. With my own children and grandchildren already established, my business closed and friends dying off, what was I supposed to do with the rest of the days that God would grant me? Now I know, and life has truly become a fight for good. I am so grateful for the big awakening that came after encountering the students in Haltern, through their letters and finally in person. I am now in a position to lessen their suffering, inherited from the atrocities committed by the Third Reich, and to plant seeds of tolerance and hope for future generations. In return, their gift to me is a renewal of purpose in my life, and each morning brings with it a new set of responsibilities and possibilities.

The children of Haltern have certainly lived up to their end of the bargain, and far exceeded any expectations. A mere six weeks after our first meeting in 1995, the students in Haltern sent me a copy of the aforementioned publication – a 108-page book that 44 students and their teachers had just completed. It chronicled what they had found in the city archives, covering the history of the Jews in Haltern, news clippings from the Nazi era, eyewitness accounts of *Kristallnacht,* and the story of the last Jewish citizens and their fates. There were articles and pictures from the vile Nazi publication, *Der Sturmer*, with caricatures of Jews, hate propaganda, Nazi laws enacted against the Jewish people, documentation of *Kristallnacht* in Haltern, and a letter that my father was forced to sign, surrendering all Jewish property to the city before the deportation. They sold this book on the marketplace at Christmastime to raise money for a memorial stone. The stone was engraved with the names of the Jewish citizens of Haltern who were murdered during the Holocaust. As previously noted, this monument now stands at the entrance to what remains of the former Jewish cemetery.

These undertakings made me realize that the students' commitment was very real. Their original invitation to me stated their interest to find out the truth. And, despite my refusal of past invitations from city officials, they wanted to hear this from me, the sole Holocaust survivor of the city. They wanted to know about my very early years - before Hitler, the hardships imposed on us during the Third Reich, and with great wonder about how I had survived. Their desire to know the truth about what had happened was indeed sincere. They were grateful that I had come to see them, knowing how difficult it was for me to return to Germany after almost 50 years. Just a few years before my visit, teaching about the Holocaust had not been allowed in German schools.

As the students began to learn this painful chapter of their history and the bloody mess they inherited, pain overwhelmed them. It was impossible for them to be in denial, as their grandfathers were, when these children confronted them. I could see their suffering as they began to bear the sins of their forefathers. It was also clear to me that they were hungry for every detail of the truth about the evil of the Nazi era.

On January 27, 1996, now the international day for commemorating the Holocaust, these same students marched through the streets with banners denouncing racism and hate. Many of them walked in the gutters, wearing the Star of David, as I was forced to do years before. This was further evidence of a connection I had created with them.

The Mayor of Haltern, Erwin Kirschenbaum and his wife, Tina, were foremost among the many friends I made there in 1995. They took a deep interest in me and kept me fully informed about the continuous work of the students at the *Realschule* during the years following that first visit. They stayed in touch by phone, email, and sent me news clippings of all subsequent projects.

What the children and good people of Haltern don't know is the degree to which they have helped me. While I cannot change history or the fact that sirens, boots, and dried leaves still bother me, at least a great deal of the pain and anger has dissipated, leaving me a better, happier, and more complete person. At least now, if something wakes me through the open window at night, such as a siren or the rustling of dried leaves similar to those that blew across the gazebo on that fateful night so many years ago, I am no longer afraid and can fall back to sleep. Now, being so much more at ease and able to turn my energies toward betterment instead of destructive hate, I realize how much the students have helped me to close a very ugly door in my own soul.

Among the projects, the class of 2000 constructed a memorial of suitcases displayed between abandoned rails at the train station to illustrate the items that the Jews could not take with them when they were forcibly relocated. It serves also to commemorate those who left and did not return. *Ort gegen das Vergessen* (the Place of No Return), has grown into so much more.

In 2001, on my second trip to Haltern, I became aware that a history teacher at the *Realschule* named Holger Freitag was acting as the advisor to students on many of their projects. These included studies and demonstrations pertaining to the Holocaust as well as current-day genocides in Bosnia, Darfur, and elsewhere. The scope of Mr.

Freitag's teachings in Haltern has helped me to incorporate the world-wide problem of genocide into my presentations to students here in Virginia.

In 2001, again due solely to the efforts of the students, the *Realschule* of Haltern was recognized by the national government in Berlin as a special school. In order to receive the honor that accompanies this recognition, there is a requirement that a "godfather" be willing to be associated with the school. It was my singular honor to be chosen as the godfather of the *Realschule*. Shortly after learning of this news, I received a letter informing me, "It would be wonderful if you could be here as the godfather when the school is honored." This was a big thing for Haltern, even if a hundred or so other schools across Germany had already earned the honor of bearing the additional name of "School Against Racism, School With Courage." And so it was that I returned to Germany alone for this trip. It was wonderful to watch the commemorative sign being passed hand to hand from person to person to me and from me back to the person who posted it to the front of the school building. It was also on this trip that I indulged myself with a trip back to my dear mother's hometown in Jever. While there, I saw her home, visited the archives at the Lutheran church, and viewed records that told of all the relatives that I never knew by name. I was also able to view a stone memorial of books that bear my maternal grandparents' names as well as those of numerous other relatives. I still find it ironic that I have all of this tangible evidence of my maternal ancestors, and yet, there is nothing for my parents or paternal grandparents. As I walked those streets, I would swear that I could feel the presence of my ancestors. It was such an emotional feeling. It was good to be in touch with them. Perhaps what made it possible was that on this trip I went back to Germany with much better feelings about Germany and myself. I had friends there and did not have the same level of distrust that I previously had harbored for so many years.

It was on the 2001 trip that Erwin Kirschenbaum and his wife Christina ("Tina") escorted me over to the college which is the home, complete with retractable dome stadium, of the great soccer team *Schalke 04*. There is also a museum attached to it that commemorates the soccer team in all of its glory, as well as all of the championship teams that have dominated the league. *Schalke 04* traces its roots back to 1904. The pictures on the wall brought back many great memories for me. I was flattered when given the complete royal treatment, and the team spokesman presented me with a commemorative *Schalke* book suitably written in with a salutation to me, as well as a hat and posters for me to take home.

· They were all very pleased to learn that all during the time I was in the concentration camps I could recall the roster of the 1934-35 league champion team. I was really hailed as a primo fan when I could still recall it sixty-six years later. The *Schalke* team was against racism. Many of the athletes were very brave and outspoken. The streets within the complex are all named for members of that championship team except for its star Fritz Szepan, who was a very big anti-Semite. Ironically, he had been one of the stars that I admired most when I was a young soccer fan.

In July of 2003, I was once again in Haltern, accompanied by my oldest son, David, and his son, Adam. I had responded to yet another letter that began, "It would be so wonderful if you could be here for the opening of the permanent memorial, *Ort gegen das Vergessen*, now contained within an original cattle car acquired by the students." People often ask me about my role in acquiring the railcar and I will again state that it was totally the work of the students – I did nothing more than show up for the dedication.

It was the day before the dedication and opening, and Erwin Kirschenbaum called Principal Weiandt to let him know that I was in town, and that I would like to come over and view the progress of things over the past two years. Before we could get over there, a small crowd had assembled and was waiting to welcome us.

It was during this meeting that I was astounded to learn the details of how the kids had found this horribly dilapidated rail car from 1908 and worked to acquire it as a permanent memorial. Looking at it brought back many memories because it was certainly of the same age and vintage as the car that had transported my family and me over the course of six days to Riga, Latvia in 1942. They had placed it on a siding of the railway station, but the city viewed it as an eyesore and refused permission for it to remain there. Not to be dissuaded, the kids and their advisors at the school decided to bring it to the school grounds. A local construction company contributed time and a crane to move the nine and one-half ton railway car. Since the railway station was going to undergo its own rehab down the road, the kids "visited" the station in the dark of night and removed a pair of rails for the car to mark its final resting place on the grounds of the school. As part of the rehabilitation project, they used new wood on the inside of the car and did an incredible job. The grounds around the car were also landscaped appropriately by the kids, and they completed the job by placing nice wood chips all around the rails. Three or four of the kids were very proud to show me what they had done to prepare the grounds. They were all grateful that I was their school's godfather. It was a wondrous feeling to share in their exultation. I never expected anyone to look up to me like that.

Imagine my amazement when I stepped into the car and found that much of the display was dedicated to my family. Included in the collection was a sign that read "A. Lebenstein" and was actually from the front of the store operated by my grandfather, Alexander, for whom I am named. According to my friend Georg Nockemann, who is a great historian, this is in fact the case. Of equal significance to me is that this sign was probably on the building when my father was himself an apprentice. They had found the sign in the attic under the rafters when they finally razed my family's house to make room for the new one that sits on the lot today. The assumption is that my father saved it after he had begun to operate the store as his own. While it was offered to me to take home to Richmond, I could not think of a more fitting resting place for it than in this railroad car where countless generations of children can respect it for the history it brings to life.

David's and Adam's reaction to all of this was utter amazement in terms of how many turned out to witness the opening of the car. Witnesses included religious leaders, civic leaders, educators, townspeople and district leaders who all wanted to be a part of it. This was also an eye-opening experience for both of them in terms of finally realizing what I had lived through when I was young.

Later during the trip, our friend Erwin Kirschenbaum took David and Adam out to a golf course driving range in Lembeck, a nearby town, where my grandfather had been born. He made introductions to some of the staff, and one of them recalled that years before there had been Lebensteins in this town too. So, after spending some time on the golf range, they went off to tour the town and found another branch of the Lebenstein family. Many years ago, these Lebenstein relatives had owned a building. The white stucco exterior of the building has been painted over many times; yet, after some sixty years, the name Lebenstein continues to bleed through the various layers of paint. Apparently the heavy oil paint used to paint the family name will not stay covered for long. It had been a small manufacturing plant that had belonged to my grandfather's relatives.

When they knocked on the door of the building, the lady who answered the door was pleased to meet other Lebensteins, and proudly displayed an old wooden coat hanger with the 'Lebenstein and Levenstein' moniker on it. Unfortunately, she would not part with it.

During this trip, both David and Adam joined me in classes of 20-25 kids and heard me speak and field questions from the classes. I think it was an eventful trip for all of us.

The greatest distinction on these subsequent trips from the first one was that I could now separate the people who perpetuated all the horrible acts from the people who are here and now. That had been the previous turmoil that tortured my soul. I could relate to the current German students in the same manner as I do with the students that I was talking to in the United States.

With the passage of time I can also now accept that most Germans were not Nazis, and there were many other German boys my age who donned the brown Hitler Youth uniform solely because they had no choice; to do otherwise would have bought them a whole bag of trouble. Having said that, I do remember the turmoil of putting a smile on my face in 1995 and facing a couple of the boys that I used to play soccer with and having the thoughts of, "Where were you when I was stuck in the *Judenhaus* for three years, or when the Nazis marched against us during *Kristallnacht*?" All of this was very painful to me.

On my trip in October 2006, my good friend Celeste accompanied me and it was intended as a private trip for the sole purpose of visiting all of our new-found friends. Naturally though, when the school learned that I was coming over, I was invited to participate in some activities, and of course to address the students one, two, or even three times. On one such visit, a couple of them grabbed both my hands and pulled me towards the cattle car and they said, "Come with us, Mr. Lebenstein;

we need your help." With nothing else said, we went outside where I was surprised to find that they had made arrangements to plant an apple tree in my honor. The hole was dug, and all was assembled to plant this tree and to dedicate it to my honor.

On this same trip, I first saw the *Stolpersteine* (stumbling stones) that had been placed in the street in front of where my home had once stood as well as those of other Jews in town at the time of *Kristallnacht*. In front of *Disselhof 36* there is a stone for each of my parents, indicating that they had lived there and then been killed during the Holocaust. A third stone is there with my name on it and reminds the reader that I am the sole survivor of the Jewish community that was consigned to the camps. While my home is gone, and on the lot where it once was stands a beautiful new building, there is a piece of the Lebensteins living on. The new building is owned by an attorney. On the inside of one of the first floor windows is a plaque that commemorates that on that particular piece of land there once existed the home and shop of the Lebensteins, and purports to tell of our history, persecution, and fate.

From the newspaper, I learned that the city had wanted to keep my family house intact, but it required so much upkeep it had fallen into disrepair. In the 1980s, an artist named Hermann Moog wanted to open a studio on the first floor and an art gallery in the second, but those plans fell through, and soon it was sold, taken down, and the new, beautiful four story building was erected on the lot.

Another noteworthy event of this 2006 trip was our sojourn to the town of Aalten, which is located about 50 miles from Haltern, just over the border in Holland. It is actually a museum that our friend, Erwin Kirschenbaum, discovered on his own, and insisted on taking us, because he thought I would find it interesting. What makes it incredibly unique is that the residents of this duplex had hidden Jews under the eaves in the attic, behind a brick wall that they had built to divide it. The irony is that in the other half of the duplex was the town's Nazi headquarters. That is courage.

At the beginning of 2007, I was pleased to receive pictures of what the most recent class at the *Realschule* had undertaken to do in an effort to commemorate the day of remembrance. This year's class had chosen to remember the 44 children who had been taken from an orphanage in the French town of Isieu and taken to a camp where they were summarily killed. To remember these children, 44 stones had been taken, cleaned, and the names of the murdered children painted on the stones. They were then placed in a circle to form a ring around my apple tree. Several blocks of ice were then set out to melt in large pans, and the water collected, drop by drop, to symbolize the tears of Isieu, which were then subsequently used to water my tree. My understanding is that this is merely the latest in the wonderful chain of events planned by the students with the help of the program coordinator, Mr. Freitag.

All of these wonderful events created such an air of cooperation among the participants. This spirit of cooperation soon took on an international flavor. Jay Ipson, co-founder of the Virginia Holocaust Museum was commenting on how he would love to have a cattle car to display at the museum but he was painfully aware of how scarce they had become over the years. He also remarked at how amazing it was that the cattle car at the *Realschule* could be an authentic one.

"I agree with you Jay, but the kids got one," I said. A week goes by, and Jay's still telling me that he does not believe that the car could be an original. I told him that it was from 1908. Another couple of weeks go by, and he asks me, "So where's the cattle car you were going to get me."

"I thought you were kidding," I said. "Do you know what it would cost?"

"Money is not an issue. You find me a car. I'll worry about transporting it."

So, I called Erwin and asked him to put out an S.O.S. to the other politicians and friends he knows to see if he could locate a car for me. He agreed. A couple of weeks go by and Erwin calls me to say that his connections had located a car, but that it would probably go fast. I told him to put a deposit down on it, and that if all else fails, that I would guarantee it. I called Jay on the 4th of July at home, and after we *kibbitzed* on a number of other topics, to include how wonderful it is to celebrate the freedom of our adopted land, I proceeded to tell him, "Oh by the way, you got your wish."

"What wish?"

"You said that you wanted a cattle car. You got your wish. Erwin found a cattle car for you, and has put a payment down on it. You want it, don't you?"

"Of course I want it. Can you help to get it over here?" asked Jay.

I then called Erwin, who looked into things and then decided that he wanted to coordinate all the logistics associated with transporting it to a ship, and in fact handled everything beautifully. If he was not a great man before, he is certainly a great man in my eyes for this good deed. Soon the car arrived in Norfolk, where it was transported to in front of the Museum where it rests today, still very much in its original state. I am grateful that I could have a small hand in bringing this piece of history to the museum for all future generations to learn from and to appreciate the dark history associated with it, and perhaps garner just a small sensation of what it would have been like to be incarcerated in such a space for six days.

CHAPTER 24

Today and Tomorrow

"We all pray to one God. I could pray with any of you, at any time, and in any place. Respect is the key."

Part of what Alex attempts to do through his work is to raise awareness regarding indifference and to spread the good that accompanies tolerance. In the course of his work, he is always looking for ways of truly reaching the one, and touching the heart. He shared one such story and did so in a manner that brought joy to the hearts of those of us who were listening.

I received a phone call from one of the staff members at the [Virginia Holocaust] Museum, suggesting that I attempt to contact a woman who had called the museum seeking assistance and guidance on how to deal with her eleven year old son. Apparently he had fallen into the company of some less than desirable boys, as well as being exposed to movies, literature or something on the Internet that prompted him to transform his bedroom into a den of hatred. His walls were covered with anti-Semitic remarks as well as numerous versions of the swastika, truly an emblem that has become a symbol of hatred and intolerance. This poor woman was so terrified that she was ready to tear her hair out. It took many phone calls before we finally connected with one another. When we finally did link up, it was only a few days before I was scheduled to depart for my 2006 trip to visit my children of the *Realschule* in Haltern, but I promised that we would get together just as soon as I returned.

After my return to Richmond, we arranged for the boy to meet me at the Holocaust Museum along with his mother and father. However, they apparently encountered some difficulty in arranging for babysitting for their two young daughters, so the father remained at home. Sizing the young boy up, I determined that all would be better served if we went to lunch and did some "bonding" before addressing the issues at hand.

While we dined at a Chinese buffet, it became obvious that the boy liked me and was enjoying himself and our time together. By the time we got back to the museum and I took him through on a very detailed tour with the intent of making him relate to the horror encountered by children of his own age at the hands of the Nazis, he was both attentive and receptive. With gratitude in the eyes of the mother, we soon parted ways.

Some days later, I received a beautiful heartfelt thank you note signed by the boy's mother that informed me that all of the hateful materials were gone from her son's bedroom, and that the loving little boy she had always known had returned. The joy and elation that I felt at that time has been multiplied with each lovely card that I receive on holidays as I am remembered by this family. If I do nothing else in this life, I changed or may have even saved one young man from a horrible life for himself, and may have in turn laid a foundation of good for future generations as he himself has children and tells them about what he learned from a Holocaust survivor.

As happened with this young man, the children will ask me questions in the course of my leading a tour or talking to them at a school that will make me think about things I have not thought about in sixty years. These questions will bring back to the forefront of my mind thoughts that I have blanked out in an effort to go on living. But once I start to think about them, there is no more rest. Like giving a computer the command to retrieve a certain piece of data, there is no stopping it.

I will go home, often exhausted, but sleep will elude me because the thoughts race through my mind. But it is my duty to continue to teach the children. We cannot be afraid of anything. When we are afraid, we defeat our own ego. Confidence is the key to success in life. Hate groups are the most afraid, which is why if you confront them, they will almost always back down. They truly are cowards and rely upon one another for reinforcement.

Most of what we encounter with hate and prejudice stems from ignorance. Ignorance as you know is nothing more than a lack of knowledge. It is nothing to be ashamed of, especially if you have never had the opportunity to know better. For this reason, it is through education that we will promote Tolerance, because I know that the Holocaust pertains to all of us. We must teach one another tolerance. We must teach one another and show one another compassion. For if we don't do these things, we are destined, no doomed, to repeat history. Because if you don't think something as horrible as the Holocaust could happen in America, you are sadly mistaken. What have we really learned from the Holocaust? Some would say absolutely nothing. Atrocities continue to this day in Africa, the Middle East, and in the form of slavery throughout many other societies. The key is to prevent any further atrocities from occurring anywhere, and to put an end to those currently being inflicted on innocent people.

If you yourself are a teenager as you read this story, odds are very good that your children will never meet a Holocaust survivor. It is up to you to teach them about tolerance and to never forget. That is your job. Hate will destroy you. It nearly destroyed me. Don't let it happen to you.

Chapter 25

Visiting in the Schools

"It is all up to you what you will do with your life. You have nobody to blame but yourself."

In the course of learning about Alex and his incredible tale of survival and the triumph of good over evil, it has been my pleasure to watch Alex visit with students of middle school, high school, and college age. Regardless of their age, the number of students in attendance, or the manner in which we are gathered, once this heroic figure of a man begins to talk, there is always quiet. As the parent of five, and grandparent of eight, it astounds me as to how captivated all of these young people become once Alex begins to tell his story of Kristallnacht and as time permits, of his battle for survival in the ghettos, concentration camps, slave labor camps, as well as his sojourn to America. At times his voice is a mere whisper and at other times, especially when relating in great detail the attack of the Nazi officer on his father and the destruction of his father's prized war medals, he is quite animated, and his booming voice echoes off the walls of the auditorium that we are typically gathered in. But before he does anything else, he always expresses gratitude for being alive, living in a free land, and the opportunity to spend some time with them. He then attempts to exact some measure of gratitude from the audience for all that they are blessed with in terms of the opportunity to receive a quality education and for all of the choices in life that they enjoy.

He then, in no uncertain terms, lets them know that they control their own destinies. Is he subtle in his approach? No way. With a smile on his face, and the practiced skill of a surgeon, he lets them have it.

"It is a beautiful day today. Not because the sun is shining in a sky so blue, but rather because we all can come to this wonderful school. We can do so in freedom. With teachers that are here to support you. You don't know how fortunate you are to have access to a library such as this, so full of books to be read and to be talked about freely. At your age, I did not know such luxuries."

"You can either make something of yourself or end up in the gutter. It is that simple. You have all that you need to accomplish wonderful things. It is your choice what you do with them all. Don't go blaming teachers, parents, or your friends. It is all up to you to decide what you will be in life; but, there really is no excuse for you to fail. The will to learn is all that is ever missing, or you are simply lazy."

After his compelling account of the events associated with Kristallnacht, it is now time for the second act. For those of us who have heard it before, we sit back waiting for the trap to be set, and the audience to be caught up in the drama as it unfolds. There is always an audible hush when he asks the question, and not rhetorically mind you, about whether he should ever go back to Germany. If the room was quiet before, it is deathly still now. Regardless of the rapport that has been established in the time leading up to this question, most in attendance will avert their eyes, especially if he attempts to solicit a response by staring intently at a student. Usually there will only be a few brave enough to raise a hand, much less find a voice, to answer the question when he says in a calm still voice, "Well? Should I go back? Should I ever go back to the country where the earth is stained with the blood of my family?"

Sometimes he will lead into this question by abruptly shattering the image that the audience has formed of a kindly older man by telling them that he was, for years and years, filled with bitter hate and anger. He will describe an unrelenting anger so bitter and so intense, that it threatened to completely overwhelm and destroy him as a person, because it was simply a force that he could not release for fear of doing great harm. "Anger related to prejudice will come to haunt you and eventually kill you," is what we have heard him say time and time again. Like a consummate thespian, he begins to really rev up, to build up a head of steam, his voice rising to a crescendo, and with this as a brilliant segue, to share what really is the best part of his entire life's story.

"Well, should I go back? What do you think? Hmm? Well?" and so it continues.

Some of the students will sit there and shout out, "No." Others will merely shake their heads as an answer. Almost always though, there is one soul brave enough to quietly utter the single word, "Yes." When this happens, Alex will pounce like a lion chasing after a gazelle in the African bush, in an effort to change the opinion of this person.

"Why should I go back to a place that killed my family, destroyed my house, did not allow me to go to school like you get to do? Why should I go back to a place that killed people like me and you simply because they were different? Black people, Jewish people, Gay people. The mentally handicapped. The physically handicapped as well. Gypsies. Literally anyone who did not have blonde hair and blue eyes? Why should I go back to that?"

"For closure," says one articulate student.

"So that you yourself can feel better," says another.

"So you can heal your heart, and get on with the rest of your life," offers another.

"Oh, so I should go back to Germany and let them make 'nice-nice' to me so that I can feel better," says Alex, slowly shaking his head, looking at his shoes, and walking across the stage as if in disbelief. For those who do not melt under his relentless attack, they are immediately rewarded by their new hero when he stops, faces them, lifts his head, smiles, and says, "Well, I went back. But only because of the children."

And thus begins his explanation of the Realschule, and all of the wonderful events that have transpired since 1995. He then encourages the kids to "Open your hearts and minds, because if you don't, intolerance will come back to haunt you."

He tells them point blank, "When you pray, pray for more than just yourself. Don't just pray for your troubles; pray for the troubles of others. Don't pray for wants, pray to give thanks. Pray for your forefathers and give thanks for them. For if they had not fought with the valor that they did, none of us would be here today. On Memorial Day and Veterans Day, step away from your picnics and celebrate the sacrifices of the brave soldiers who fought for our freedom. Celebrate Freedom! Pray for the children that inherited such a bloody awful mess from their grandfathers."

Why does Alex push himself as hard as he does? Why isn't he sitting on his patio enjoying the flowers and warm Virginia weather of his retirement? He answers this question in a quiet voice with a tinge of sadness.

"My age group does not have the guts to do what is right. They have made such a mess of things, and I am only sorry that they have dumped such a mess of garbage on the children of this new generation, and because it can happen here if we are not very very careful. We need to do all that we can to prevent the new generation from developing any prejudice. Does a child really know right from wrong? It is up to the parents, teachers and religious leaders to instill the proper values in the children of today and of future generations. There is a little bit of God in all of us. The challenge is to work on the good that is inside of you and to ignore the bad."

What makes Alex continue to work sometimes until two o'clock in the morning returning e-mails to students, teachers, and other interested people with his one-finger hunt and peck method of keyboarding? What makes him continue to spend "his children's inheritance" in this educational crusade? The answer is always the same: the children.

"When I pray in the morning, I do so merely to give thanks. I know that I am so lucky to be alive that I do not pray for anything more. I do not pray to be given anything else. I pray simply for all that I have already been given.

This is the best thing that has ever happened to me. I'm okay, you're okay. I may not be completely healed – I may never be; but what I do know is that I am a lot healthier emotionally today than I have ever been at any point in my life."

And when we ask him whether he in turn takes solace and courage from the children, his answer is just a broad smile.

CHAPTER 26

Odds and Ends

I am often asked little things, like: When was the first time you did this or did that? When did you attend your first baseball game? Are you a Republican or a Democrat? What kind of music do you like? Why people want to know these things certainly escapes me. For some reason however, lots of people want to know when and how I learned to drive a car. Well, it is actually an amusing little story which spans more than a couple of years.

As a young boy, all I had been exposed to within my own household was a horse and buggy or a bicycle. The first time I ever drove a motor vehicle of any kind was when we first escaped from our Russian liberators and the hospital in Danzig. I was with my two friends, Ewald and Zompka, and I was making a valiant attempt at driving if for no other reason than to impress them that I was as worldly as they. Naturally, the car was equipped with a manual transmission, and it kept bucking like crazy, and of course, as a result, I was stalling it out. This severely frustrated my friend Zompka who would say, "Get out of here snot nose, let me drive," and with that he would shove me aside and take the wheel. Not to be dissuaded, I attempted to drive on another occasion, unfortunately with the same result, never quite mastering the concept of clutch and gas. Again Zompka berated me, and with, "You don't know how to drive. You're going to kill us all. Get in the back. I'll drive," ringing in my ears I humbly crawled in the back, and decided I would try again later, without Zompka in attendance! Those were my first attempts.

My next attempts did not take place until after I had arrived in the United States, and had been here about 18 months, and was already in Florida. I applied for a job at the Crossroads restaurant. They had a separate commissary some distance away, and we would do the portion control work at the commissary and then load the truck with trays to be taken to the restaurant. In the course of my interview I was asked, "Do you know how to drive this truck?" and my natural response was, "Of course I know how to drive." Well, let's just say that there is a set of gears and transmission that would probably argue this point with me.

With that, the interview is over, and he tells the assistant chef to take me over to the commissary which was about a mile away. All the deliveries and portion control were done there. So the guy shows me the lay of the land, and instructs me on my duties. It all seems pretty straight forward, except for driving the truck. It was a ¾ ton truck with built-in shelves for deliveries. He tosses me the keys, and never asks me if I have a driver's license. It was definitely a different day and age than it is today. He then tells me to load the truck and to take the food over to the restaurant. Driving to the restaurant from the commissary was quite an adventure and I stalled the truck out more times that I can count, but somehow managed to get there. The next day was a light day, yet I was slow in getting out of the commissary with the delivery. So I jump into the truck, and despite my best efforts, I keep bucking and stalling the engine. The cops finally pull me over because I am holding up traffic! By the time I buck for three more blocks, I am finally getting the hang of it, and soon I can safely navigate the streets without tying up traffic. Fortunately, the following days were progressively better, and I became smooth in operating the truck.

I never went to driving school, but eventually self taught, I got licensed. This was shortly before I bought my first car in anticipation of getting married. My first car was a used Dodge, and after manipulating that truck around, a regular car was a piece of cake. I still enjoy driving today, and do appreciate the luxury of an automatic transmission.

CHAPTER 27

That the Children Will Know

"I won't stop until I drop."

A few things that Alex has taught us is that it is okay to be different, but it is never okay to be indifferent. Faith does not have to be perfect it merely needs to be sincere. As the aches and pains and other limitations of age begin to make themselves more apparent, he remembers to say his prayers, and reads from his own scriptures daily, and always remembers to address God with gratitude in his heart by reciting: "I gratefully thank you O living and eternal king, for You have restored my soul within me with compassion – abundant is your faithfulness."

I am one hundred percent American. The only reason that I ever go back to Germany now is to help my children. It astounds me that I have gone from wanting to kill these children out of pure hatred to considering them my children. I will not hesitate now to refer to them as my children, to include those I have not even met yet. I have no hope for my generation, be they German or American. I know how hard it is to be free of prejudice. We have messed things up way too badly. Our only hope is the children. Everybody has some feelings of prejudice within them. I doubt if we will ever be free of this destructive force.

I want the black community to wake up so badly that we should all live in harmony, just as I would love to see Israel and the Arabs to live in harmony side by side. Even my own children's generation is too far prejudiced.

My goal is to try to prevent the younger generation from developing these same prejudices. I am working very hard to insure that the young ones understand that prejudice starts in the home and only continues in the school and school yard if not checked.

I will watch for someone wearing an expensive pair of sneakers. I will then ask them if they would make fun of somebody else who might be wearing a ratty old pair of torn worn out sneakers. If they say yes, then I jump on them, and point out that they are being prejudiced. What if they can't afford anything better? What if that person has a good heart and is a good person? What if the only thing that they are guilty of is not having enough money for expensive sneakers? I then tell this person that if they don't see that they are prejudiced about something as simple as a pair of sneakers, then they are on the wrong track already. I try to reduce the conversation to as low a level, or as low a common denominator, as possible so that they can understand.

I cannot correct the world. I know I can't and have no intention of trying to do so. But that doesn't mean that I am not going to try to reach one person at a time. That is my privilege, and that is what I want to do. It makes me feel good, especially after what I went through when I was their age. If I can send a message to that kid with the good sneakers and send him home thinking about what we talked, chances are that he will become best buddies with that kid with the worn out sneakers. The sneakers then become an object lesson. And if they can become buddies, others can too. That is the whole purpose of what I do, and none of this could ever be happening if I had not gone back. I was one of the most prejudiced angry people you could ever have met. It is nothing short of a miracle that I am even alive.

I still encounter people who do not believe that I am a Holocaust survivor. There are very few of us who have been able to do something positive with our experiences. Elie Wiesel is one. I admire him so much for what he has been able to do. Not to forget, but to put anger on the shelf, and to raise a family. Most children of Holocaust survivors face challenges because of baggage being hauled around by their parents.

My new life really began when I was sixty-eight years old. Until then, I was living with this horrible inner turmoil. My anger would come out in the form of my snapping at people, having to be in control, especially in business. To this day, I cannot allow anyone to dominate me. I am my own person. I am not looking for anything more or anything less than being equal. I guess it is more a matter of not wanting to hear that someone feels that he is better than me.

My previous outlook on life was that it was all a fight. Nothing had ever come easy to me. I was willing to work hard and to fight for everything that I earned or claimed as my own. Now, I am fighting for something totally different. I see a light at the end of the tunnel. It is a whole new experience for me. I experienced a great awakening when I met those kids in Germany. From the time of the first trip, I did not leave Germany with the same anger. While I would never accept German citizenship or want to live there, or have to adopt it as my primary language even though it was my mother tongue, I do feel so much better towards the children.

At this point in my life, I am more concerned with showing gratitude to God for all that I have been blessed with in my life, rather than asking for more, because I simply have no need for more. I cannot express how grateful I am to be a father, a grandfather, and great-grandfather. You can't weigh family against anything else. While I still miss my own parents – after all, I lost them at age fourteen – I definitely feel God's blessings whenever I am around my own family.

I also know that what I am doing now is simply my duty and my calling. I am one of the last survivors. I must tell my story. I also believe that the world needs "straightening up" in a big way and it will have to be the younger generation that accomplishes it, for it is definitely up to the children that I am teaching now to restore peaceful co-existence to the world.

As long as I have strength, good health, and God's permission, I will continue to speak out to the children of the world so that they in turn can raise up the next generation with greater feelings of tolerance.

While I feel more complete now, I don't know if I could say that I am at peace now. The world is still a very dangerous place. I am now an old man. I would be lying if I said that I did not harbor my own prejudices. But as I awaken each day, I realize that it is up to me to make a difference, albeit in some small way, and that I need to wrestle with my own prejudices in order to be a good example to my children, so that they in turn can raise up an entirely new generation of even more righteous children, where the lamb and the lion can in fact lay down together to bring peace to this world.

My goal for the remaining time that I am blessed with is to keep it rolling over with the children, both here and in Germany. It is important to me that the children know, and that they are in a position to tell their own children. I often remind them that they will be the last generation to meet a Holocaust survivor.

And when I wake up tomorrow, I will give thanks to God for letting me awake, for my abundance, and for all of my daily blessings. And I will let Him know that he has returned my soul within me...

CHAPTER 28

Fan Mail

Over the course of the past ten years, Alex has received literally thousands of thank you notes and letters written by students from dozens of schools in the United States as well as from the City of Haltern in Germany. In the short time that we have been accompanying him on his visits, we have seen the gratitude with which the children will cling to him after his presentation, hungering for more of his time and more of his words.

From the Children

Dear Mr. Lebenstein:

I was one of the students [I am a senior (12th grade)] who attended the presentation at the Holocaust Museum the day you delivered your message. After I heard your story, I could not get you out of my mind and heart. There is so much I would love to tell you, but I find myself at a loss for words.

Since I was a small girl, I have studied the events of the Holocaust. I have seen "Schindler's List" as well as Mr. Spielberg's recent documentary of Holocaust survivors. I have read several books including *The Diary of Anne Frank* and Corrie Ten Boom's *The Hiding Place*. Of all these, however, it has been your story that has influenced me the most. I cannot remove your words from my thoughts.

Mr. Lebenstein, may I encourage you to *never* stop telling your story. The power in the truth of your experience has given me the desire to tell as many as possible about this horrific time in our world's history. To make them aware of the brutality of man when left to himself and that it is in *division* that the most traumatic of suffering can occur – that of the heart, mind and body.

In a short time, a few years perhaps, I will have children of my own. Though they will never, as you said, hear about the Holocaust first-hand and though you will never meet them, I feel it is my duty and honor, which I will gladly embrace, to share with them your story. It was my immense privilege to meet you. Whether you realize it or not, you have passed on your life's story to a new generation. Thank you for sharing with us despite the difficulty. It has left a life-long impression on my heart. May the Lord bless you and keep you.

P.S. The theater class at my school is performing a short play on the Holocaust. In this drama, I portray the character of a nun hiding children in a convent. Your testimony has given me a new perspective and passion for my character. Thank you.

Humble Regards,
C.W., High School student

Dear Mr. Lebenstein:

Recently, you related to students of our high School your personal account of the Holocaust. I was very fortunate to be a part of that audience. Along with the impacting details of some well-known historical events, I was moved and mesmerized by the words you spoke about your experiences like hiding in the graveyard to buying the cake for your peers. Those who had arrived blind to the prejudices of the world before the speech definitely received a powerful insight into the many terrors you and thousands of others experienced because of cruelty.

Previous to the speech, I considered myself to be rather open-minded to all religions, races, etc. However, after your presentation, I realized I too needed to become less narrow-minded. Thank you for opening my eyes to the truth and the unfortunate harshness of reality. I will always remember such a captivating speech that not only opened my eyes but my heart. Your presence was a privilege for all who could attend.

Sincerely,
M.R., High School student

Dear Mr. Lebenstein:

Rarely in one's life can one individual witness history before their very own eyes, yet be so fortunate to spend a Thursday morning with not only a Holocaust survivor, but also a wonderful person. I greatly appreciate you taking the time and traveling up to Cherry Hill to share your story with us. In gratitude to you, I am now more grateful of life itself, and understand how lucky I am to live in this wonderful country during this extraordinary time period. It is amazing how a one-hour class discussion can give you a different perspective of exactly the true meaning of life.

Although I am not a Jewish child, I can relate myself to your situation. Like you, I am very close to my family and cherish all the times we spend together. You can never know when this love may end and how long they will be with my physically, albeit they will always be in my heart. Several years ago I too lost several important people of my family, and I understand exactly how hard it is to move on. And in spite of the fact that I didn't suffer with unjust rules under a man we all despise, your powerful and self-moving speech gave me a precise feeling of exactly how life was in the horrific concentration camps.

Mr. Lebenstein you are a hero in my mind's eye and your strength and determination to withstand that pain and the hurt is truly remarkable. To be the sole survivor of the forty-seven families of your hometown in Haltern is an inspiration to us all. It is evident that you matured quickly since those tragic times and this were able to build a wonderful family.

It is hard to single out one particular thing I liked most from your presentation. However, I was especially interested by the book you prepared after your experiences. It gave me a look at how the Jews were awfully tortured and a sense of great hate for the Nazis. And as you constantly repeated, we here at our school are the future of America. To advance into the near future and avoid such terrible persecution, we have to learn about our past. As disappointing as that may be.

Sincerely,
B.Y., Middle school student

Dear Mr. Lebenstein,

I'd like to start by saying that no small words of mine can ever express the deep debt of gratitude I owe you for sharing your experience with me.

Before yesterday, I only had a vague picture of what it was like in those desperate times. Now, I can almost see it clearly enough to know that I can prevent this from happening again. Thank you for giving me even a small morsel of hope that all this hatred can maybe one day be erased. That was probably the one thing I will remember even when I have grandchildren.

I realize that I can never imagine the pain and mental anguish that you and so many others suffered. I understand that your view of the world will always be unique. Your experience touched me in a way that nothing else could because you helped me to understand that I should enjoy my life the way it is because there was a time when people couldn't even walk on the sidewalks.

I will always admire you for your courage to stand up and tell about what happened. It made me think about my own heritage: my grandmother's mother was a twin and they had a big family in Poland. The family sent my great-grandmother to the States to have a better life. She kept in touch with her twin until just before the war ended, when they disappeared without a trace. Nobody ever found out what happened to them. I'm glad that at least you know what happened. Sometimes I tell myself that I'll find out what happened one day, but then I realize that they searched for years and never found anything. They think that they were murdered by Germans.

Is it okay if I e-mail you sometime? I'd like to learn more. Thank you so much for your time.

Sincerely,

J.H., Middle school student

Dear Mr. Lebenstein:

Like all of the other students who were present when you came to our school to talk to us, I would like to thank you from the bottom of my heart ☺. It's not very often that a student who is learning about the Holocaust has the chance to actually meet and talk to a survivor. It was very nice of you to take the time to specially visit our school. I know it must be hard to talk about some of the most traumatic points of your life, but you did it to teach us some things that we did not know. Like you said, we are very fortunate and we really should be thankful for what we have, and are living like today.

I was very grateful for how you openly and honestly expressed your emotions. I learned a lot from your speech and I hope I always remember the valuable lessons you taught me. The horrible Nazis had no right to treat you, along with all of the other victims of the Holocaust, so unjustly and cruelly. Your statement was very true that it's up to the people today to make sure that something like that never happens again. Your brought tears to my eyes from describing how you suffered so mentally and emotionally. Again, I deeply appreciate your visit and will always remember it for the rest of my life. ☺

Yours truly,

P.S., Middle school student

P.S. Thanks for the generous donation of the book!

Dear Mr. Lebenstein:

I would like to show my gratitude to you for coming to share your story with my class. What you told us was very enlightening, and it helped me to better understand what people went through during those trying times. I have read books about the Holocaust before, but having an actual survivor come and share his experiences with me makes everything I've ever read about come to life. What you have told me is invaluable, and it is something I will always carry with me. I know that it was emotionally hard for you to relate your story to my class, but I feel that what you have done will help the young people of today realize how important racial and cultural tolerance really is. I know the effects of prejudice are lasting on you, and I am sure they are for other people. Sharing your time with us helped me to realize that.

I cannot imagine what it would be like for a young boy to go through what you did when you were young. I am sure that it has greatly changed your life, and I admire you for coming forward and telling your story. Although it is a painful one, your story is important and needs to be shared, not only because some people deny the Holocaust ever happened, but because it is a story that teaches. It has made me aware of the effects that acts of prejudice can have on a person, no matter what the size of the act. Of course, I could learn this lesson through a book or a movie, but hearing the testimony of an actual Holocaust survivor, a privilege not many people will have, makes it that much more real to me, not to mention more memorable.

Sincerely,
C.M., High school student

Dear Mr. Lebenstein:

I really enjoyed and appreciated you coming and speaking to my English class. I realized that you have experienced many different hard times, and many battles have come your way but as time has passed you have overcome them. I know as a student it must be very hard for you to come and tell your life story to us debating how we will take it. I was very touched and so a lot of gratitude. There are not many words that can express and show you how much I appreciate you speaking but I feel like just as a phoenix rises from the ashes you have risen from a man who looked at the world with hatred. To a man who realizes that no one should be treated like that and also a man who can talk about it and hope to touch someone else's life.

Thank you for donating your time.

Sincerely,

A.S., High school student

From the Adults

"Alex made some a huge impression upon the city with his several visits, that I cannot walk through the streets of Haltern without someone stopping me and asking me if I have heard from Alex and whether he is well."

- Erwin Kirschenbaum, friend and former
Burgermeister (Mayor) of Haltern am See

"I first met Alex last winter at a teacher workshop here at the Virginia Holocaust Museum. Alex graciously offered to speak at my school and I organized what I affectionately called "Alex Day." He came to James River High School and spoke to a group of nearly a thousand students. Those of you familiar with teenagers know that they can be a tough audience. During assemblies, they usually fidget, sleep, or whisper to each other, but from the moment Alex began to speak the students were riveted. He had them right in the palm of his hand for ninety minutes. Now, THAT is truly a gift!

I'd like to share one specific story of that day. I had a seventeen year old student who had recently transferred from Florida. He always wore black, had a shaved head, and was extremely serious. As we learned about the Holocaust in my class, he remained cautiously interested, and one day admitted to me that before moving to Virginia, he had been a member of a white supremacist gang but was now willing to hear the other side.

After Alex's assembly, the students were able to come to the library during their lunch periods to interact with him on a more personal level.

Over the course of four lunches, at least 400 students came and went. They swarmed Alex like a rock star, having their pictures taken with him and asking for his autograph. But my serious young student stayed back and watched and waited. I saw that he was getting emotional and asked if he was okay. He said yes, but he really wanted to speak to Alex. I took him closer, and Alex gave him his undivided attention, and they shared a private conversation. The boy began to cry and Alex embraced him and gave him his business card in case he ever needed to reach him.

Later in the day, after Alex had gone home, the young man came to see me, still crying. He told me that he was ashamed of how he had lived his life and that Alex had shown him the truth. He no longer wanted to live with hatred and anger. He said, "Alex is a man of honor and that's what I want to be." Well, when he turned eighteen in July, he joined the U. S. Marines and became that man of honor.

Alex, you truly are a hero to many, but to me, you are an angel.

-Jackie Tully, Midlothian High School,
Midlothian, VA

EPILOGUE

Full Circle: Sorrow and Triumph

"My entire experience of those two weeks was colored by the overwhelming emotions that I experienced in those fields of stones in the forests of Riga."

We had pretty much finished the fifth or sixth draft of the book and were working on the nitty-gritty of his incredible life story when Alex called to say that he had just received a letter from the City of Haltern. The letter stated that the City wanted him to return to Haltern yet again for a very special purpose. The city wanted to recognize Alex with a ceremony at which he would be recognized as an Ehrenburger, or honored citizen. Alex of course expressed some reticence when he heard the word "citizen." Calls to Germany revealed that this award was not anything to do with granting any form of citizenship but rather a declaration on the part of the City that Alex would become an "especially honored person of the City of Haltern." We then talked about it at length, and as we discussed the significance of this honor in terms of those that Alex continues to serve, the question became moot. Of course he would accept the honor, with the same grace and spirit as he has embraced the children of this new generation, and furthered his

241

work towards rearing a generation that will embrace tolerance of those who are different than themselves.

The significance of this honor became even more apparent when we learned that Alex would be the first recipient in over fifty years to receive the title of Ehrenburger.

Even more amazing than the declaration of Alex's status as an honored person was the proposed re-naming of the Stadtlische Realschule to the Alexander Lebenstein Realschule, School Against Racism, School With Courage. We were ecstatic for him. We could not envision a more fitting honor and lasting tribute for both Alex and the work he has done over the years in providing service to the children of the city. Plans began to be made. At the same time, we also thought: what a wonderful way to finish the book since the work continues! Could there be any more fitting way to end this remarkable story?

Many hours went into preparing a suitable itinerary. Scheduling conflicts would prevent Susie and I from making the trip, but Alex was nonetheless accompanied by a large entourage of family and friends from the United States to include a videographer who would capture the festivities in Haltern on behalf of the Virginia Holocaust Museum.

In addition to the week in Haltern, Alex decided that he was going to first make his long awaited pilgrimage to Riga, Latvia so that he could finally honor his parents in person. His past efforts to get there had all been delayed or postponed due to health concerns or scheduling conflicts. He would also lead a select group of students from the Realschule to Berlin, Germany where they would be able to continue their studies of the Holocaust under the tutelage of their school's godfather. It was an ambitious itinerary and one that worried all of us because of its exhausting nature, but Alex was not to be dissuaded. Memorial Day, 2008 was the scheduled departure for this odyssey.

I was certainly concerned, if not darn right overwhelmed, at the thought of accepting any form of citizenship. While I am still eligible to this day to apply for German citizenship, I could not imagine ever doing so. Naturally when I heard the word citizen I was concerned that I would have to re-live the painful decision of 1945 when I determined that I would never again be a German citizen. Fortunately it was then explained to me just what this honor really meant to me, the city, and ultimately my children at the *Realschule*. Naturally, I was both humbled and appreciative of the honor that was being bestowed upon me.

The Forests of Riga

The forests surrounding the city of Riga are now quiet, even tranquil. The wind blows threw the trees and the birds that occupy their branches break the eerie silence that surrounds the numerous memory stones that have been placed in remembrance of the countless victims. The forest is a bird sanctuary today but the stones are grim reminders of when the trees were a canopy to ghastly killing fields. Thousands of people, mainly Jews, were brought to these forests from the Riga Ghetto, herded from the trains and trucks and then chased to the edge of a large pit, many still not knowing what was to be their fate. Many of these pits had been dug by forced labor and in some instances by their intended occupants. The peace of the forest would then be shattered by the sound of machine gun fire as these innocent souls were killed in a hail of bullets, finally to rest in a mass grave together. Today these mass graves are grass covered mounds that in most cases have a retaining wall of concrete around them to help identify and consecrate the ground.

Rumbula and Bikernieki

Two separate forests located about six miles apart as they ring the city of Riga. Anyone familiar with the history of World War Two and the Holocaust know of their notoriety. Alex visited both hallowed sites, as he humbly remembered his parents and all of the victims who perished in both locations. A visitor to these somber sites is met by large stones placed in the grounds with no set plan or arrangement. Engraved on these stones are the names of those who were unfortunate to perish there. Surviving family members have insured that they are not forgotten.

243

Because the living have an obligation to escort the soul of their beloved deceased loved ones, it is tradition to erect a monument to these departed family members. If in fact a monument is erected, this lifetime obligation is deemed fulfilled. Now, it is quite common to acknowledge subsequent visits to the grave site by leaving a small stone on top of the erected monument.

Watching the video of Alex walking among the stones, fruitlessly looking for the names of his parents, softly reading the names and talking to his parents, is both heartbreaking and nearly traumatizing to the viewers.

It is like stepping on holy ground. The memorials have language engraved that indicate that we should never forget; that the spilled blood of innocents' should not be covered up, and that we should all be able to hear the screams. Even now, I can imagine the screams that accompanied the painful last moments of so many people. This will be the last time that I will ever come here. Rumbula and Bikernieki. The mere mention of their names is enough to make me sad. So many stones, so many stones. Ach, so many names of innocent people who died for no crime other than that of being Jewish or different in some other way. Are they not all my parents, my brothers and sisters, all so brutally murdered in the name of hate?

I could not find my parents' names on any of the stones, but I know they are here. Years ago I paid to have their names added to the stones that have been placed in a tribute to all of the innocents who lost their lives here. I wandered around and around but could not find my parents. But I know that they are here. Soon I discovered a wild lilac bush growing near one of the graves, and I began to feel my mother. I have to believe that it is where my mother was buried. She loved lilacs, and I am sure that this was her way of letting me know where she is resting. It was so overwhelming that my mind went absolutely numb. I mouthed the *kaddish* (memorial prayer) but the words were leaden, and my heart was absolutely breaking. It was as if I was losing my mother all over again.

We soon left the forests, and saw more of Riga. I walked at the railway station Skirotava which is still marked the same way as it was in January 1942 when my parents and I arrived in a cattle car as part of the transport at the end of our five and a half day odyssey. The sights and sounds of the station had a peculiar effect on me. I almost began feeling the same anxiety that I had when my feet first touched the ice-covered cobblestones oh so many years ago when I was a mere boy.

The three days that I spent in Riga were important. I am glad that I finally was able to visit my parents and to pay my respects to them. I just didn't realize how this trip to Riga, particularly to the forests, was going to impact me. To say that it absolutely blew me away for the duration of the trip would be a gross under statement. I had been home for two months and I still felt as if I needed to "snap out of it." What nobody realized is that I was nearly to the point where I needed professional help. I then received a call to speak at a school. It was again the children that proved to be my remedy and the balm that allowed me to overcome my pain.

Berlin

It was my privilege to leave Riga by plane and to meet 24 students and 3 teachers from the Haltern *Realschule* in the capital city of Berlin, Germany. They represented the graduating class of the school, and were instrumental in leading the school in the teaching of tolerance. They not only set the curriculum in regard to Holocaust studies but expanded it to include tolerance in general and the support of those in need. The area of focus this year (2008) had been Australia. I am very proud of their awareness of what is going on in the world around them and the fact that they can consider studying about places like Australia or as in years past, Darfur, to understand the significance that intolerance and indifference can play in destroying a society or a people.

In Berlin, we visited the newly re-opened *Reykerstrasse* Synagogue and were able to partake in Friday night services. The focal point of our trip was the opportunity to tour and study the literature and pictures of the Nazi archives at the *Wannsee* Museum. As you may recall, *Wannsee* was the very place that the plans for the annihilation of the Jewish race, otherwise known as the Final Solution, had its origin. While it added even more heaviness to my heart to view all of the reminders of this horrible time in my life, I was gratified to be doing it with the children of my school. It actually hurt me to watch them experience the pain and the shame associated with the legacy left to them by their grandparents as they went about learning just exactly what heinous acts were committed in the name of racial purity or *lebensraum*.

I also remember having the conscious thought that anyone who still maintains that the Holocaust never occurred merely has to walk through the halls of *Wannsee* to know that it most certainly did happen and that countless millions of lives were lost in the name of madness. With the same efficiency that marked the killing performed by the Nazis while they were in power, the proof contained in these archives is most thoroughly documented for all to see. It is my prayer, as I and the remaining survivors continue to die and depart this Earth, the world will never forget the madness of this time, and that *Wannsee* will remain a focal point for learning from this madness so that it is never repeated.

Another high point of the trip to Berlin for me was the opportunity to bring closure to another chapter of my life that dates back to the fateful days of *Kristallnacht*. For over four years, I had been in contact with a woman who was making inquires on behalf of her father who had attended school with me in Haltern. During several of my previous trips I had suggested that we get together with her father so that we could meet face to face, but it never happened. Each time I suggested it there was yet another excuse. This time however, when I suggested it, he agreed.

When we were attempting to reconcile our calendars and I mentioned that I had a previous engagement for the luncheon time that he proposed, he invited our entire party to lunch. Today this man is a respected professor and doctor, and has accomplished much with his life. Back in 1938, he was a snot-nosed kid like me and unfortunately happened to be the son of a very active and vocal local Nazi leader. Undoubtedly his father scripted him to join one of the hate groups that I encountered during my younger years. While I cannot remember for certain, it stands to reason that he would have been one of those brown-shirted boys who attacked me in front of my home on the second day of *Kristallnacht*. The pain in his eyes when we met and we recounted my chronicle of the war years touched both of us very deeply and I realized anew that there were victims of all kinds during the war. His shame, his embarrassment, the manner in which he held his head in his hands reminded me of the importance of being able to distinguish between the criminals of that era and the poor hapless people who were often swept up into the madness as unwilling participants only desiring to survive themselves. I must say that I not only marveled at his reactions to our conversation, but also my own. I did not feel anything but compassion for this man who had to come to terms with not only with his own actions, in all likelihood dictated to him by his father, but more tragically, those of his father. I know that if our roles were reversed and I had to learn that my dear father had been guilty of the heinous crimes that his father undoubtedly was, it would be incredibly painful for me to reconcile such a thing in my heart.

One thing that did make it easier for me while in Berlin was the presence of my friend and associate Georg Nockemann. Georg had driven from Haltern solely to be with me in Berlin and to provide the additional moral support that he wisely knew that I would need. This faithful friend never left my side as we toured this powerful collection of history.

Ehrenburger

It was soon time for Georg to drive us back to Haltern so that we could engage in the activities for which I had returned to Germany. Despite my best efforts to do so, I was unable to shake the heavy feeling of gloom that had settled on my heart. Walking through the forests of Riga and being that much closer to my dear parents had certainly taken a far greater toll than I could ever have imagined. It was probably unwise to have added that segment of the journey to what really was meant to be a time of happiness and celebration, but I felt that it was my duty to finally go there after all these years and to pay homage to my parents.

Upon our arrival in Haltern, we were taken to the *Hotel Am Turm* which is located next to the last surviving of the seven devil towers (turm) dating back to the 16th century. One of the best things about staying at this hotel is its proximity to everything in town. Being located in the center of the city, we were able to walk to the City Hall, the railroad station, as well as to the school.

Wednesday, the fourth day of June, was truly a momentous day in my life. In the morning I was able to sit in the courtyard of the *Realschule* and in three groups of four hundred students, I was able to have breakfast with my children. This was a special occasion and was catered by the school in anticipation of what was going to happen that evening at City Hall and the next day back at the school. It was wonderful to partake of good food with all of those bright and eager young people all around me.

That afternoon I was honored to spend time in the home of Waldemar and Monika Plum, the son of Anne Plum (nee Sondermann). The Plums were the family that had operated the old hotel in which we had been provided refuge from the bitter cold and the atrocities of the cemetery during the night of *Kristallnacht*. That hotel has since been converted into condominiums which precipitated our stay at the new hotel. It was good to spend some quiet time in the company of good people who I have counted as friends for many years now.

Before I knew it, the appointed hour for the evening's activities had arrived, and it was time for us to leave our hotel rooms and to venture over to the city hall. The degree of pomp and circumstance that accompanied the ceremony was overwhelming to all of my senses. It was only after I had been home in Richmond, Virginia and able to view a tape recorded version of the ceremony several times that I was able to begin to grasp just what a huge honor it is in being declared an *Ehrenburger*. What made it even more incredible is that it had been over fifty years since the previous presentation.

Now, to be completely honest, I know that there were many in the community that thought it was inappropriate for me to be declared an honored person of Haltern given the fact that I neither reside there nor did my services to the students at the school benefit the lives of everyone in the town. Certainly those with enrolled students would be benefitted, but this was not representative of everyone in the town. In any event, the decision was made to bestow the honor upon me, and I was bound and determined to use it to promote my message of tolerance.

The ceremony was very touching as the *Burgermeister,* Bodo Klimpel, and several other dignitaries addressed the elite group assembled. Apparently simply being *invited* to this ceremony is testimony of the esteem and status in which a person is held. Numbered among these celebrated members of the community were the same twenty four students and three teachers from the graduating class of the *Realschule* that I had accompanied during their studies in Berlin.

The actual certificate that declares me to be an honored person is an oversized document in a large heavy cardboard frame with the signatures of the city's officials, past and present, on a facing document. All in all a very impressive looking document.

Adding to the special nature of the night was that I was joined by my fellow survivors Ewald Aul and Rolf Abramson, as well as Maaike Thomas, Monica Plum, and Annette Fluester. These three ladies have been with me every time I have visited since 1995 and have organized many beautiful events. My good friends Erwin and Tina Kirshenbaum interrupted their vacation in Scotland and flew back solely to attend the ceremony that night. It was very touching to me and makes me realize just how blessed I truly am to enjoy the friendships I do.

The ceremony itself lasted a little over an hour and was very impressive indeed. I am grateful that I now to get to re-live it on video and take in all that I missed during that overwhelming experience. Following the ceremony there was a huge display of delicacies on which we were able to dine to include fish, cheese, *wursts* (sausages), and an abundant supply of beer and wine.

Of course when I view the tapes of the ceremony and the festivities, I can still feel the emotions of Riga that weighted down my heart that day. I felt like my acceptance speech was not up to par and certainly not what I had envisioned delivering. What should have been a day filled with joy and laughter was something much less than that for me as I had conscious thoughts of my parents and how different our lives could have been had my father made any number of alternative decisions during my childhood.

The Alexander Lebenstein Realschule

Thursday was another big day for me. From late morning until mid-afternoon I was at the school that from that day forward would bear my name. At 1100, a rabbi from the nearby town of Recklinghausen, where a Jewish community and synagogue has been restored, was brought in to pronounce a special prayer in honor of my parents who had been so brutally murdered. I greatly appreciated this thoughtful gesture. The prayer he recited was a *mole rachamim*, or prayer of remembrance. As he said it I felt myself drifting back to Riga yet again and all the sights and sounds of the previous week. The entire experience had served to take me back too many years, and I realize, even at the time of this writing, that it is important for me to immerse myself in my work and to put this behind me or it could still consume me.

The program was full of singing, speeches, readings, all under the direction of the music director, Maria Curti. Some of it was in English, some in German, but all of it was done in the proper spirit of love and cooperation. To this end, the leaders of the two leading churches in the city, namely Catholic and Lutheran, stood side by side, united in the events of this day. I was so struck by the fact that they were standing there, ostensibly honoring the lone surviving Jew of the town, that I mentioned it good-naturedly in my remarks.

As speeches were made, and people were praising me for my courage, it was all I could do to sit there quietly taking in the degree of emotion that was accompanying the events of the day. I was being praised for my work of the past thirteen years in helping the students to understand what tolerance really is, and how they need to incorporate it into all facets of their lives.

In what felt like a blink of an eye, the time flew by and soon it was time to go outside to unveil the new name on the school. Even now, some months after the event, it still seems so surreal to see my name on the front of the school. Not bad for a kid with only three years of formal education past kindergarten! I had no sooner pulled down the cloth covering the large metal letters that twelve beautiful doves were released and soared into the sky much in the same manner as my heart did at that moment.

Imagine my surprise when I learned that there is no record of a school being named for a living person. The balance of the afternoon was a time of celebration even if my heart was not fully invested.

The Cemetery

As part of the video that I wanted to assemble for the Virginia Holocaust Museum, we ventured to the old Jewish cemetery on the outskirts of town where my parents and I had hidden ourselves on that fateful night of *Kristallnacht*. As previously noted, two thirds of it, to include the graves of my grandparents is now covered by the highway. The ravine where we hid ourselves is still there, and when I carefully lowered myself down in the grass for purposes of capturing it on video it was almost as if I could relive the terror of that night.

The Green Party

On Thursday evening, my three friends, Maaike Thomas, Monika Plum, and Annette Fluester hosted a wonderful dinner party for my family and friends as well as the dignitaries that had participated in the previous events. It was held at a natural farm located outside of town. It was asparagus harvest time, and we were treated to the most delightful fresh asparagus soup, asparagus prepared in an old-fashioned German way, other fresh vegetables, as well as good traditional German beer.

Muenster

On Friday we ventured over to the city of Muenster. I was actually down in a long tunnel under the railroad station where another exhibit had been established to honor the memory of those who had been shipped on a transport from the town destined for the Riga ghetto. While down there, we ran into a tour group consisting of twenty five young people aged 18-22 years. Their leader recognized me and asked if it would be possible for me to make a presentation to the group. Before I knew it I had found my voice and had delivered a 25 minute presentation without my interpreter. This presentation was also captured on video. The students were in awe and greatly appreciated the opportunity to meet an actual Holocaust survivor.

Dinner

As if the entire week had not been an absolute dream, my friends once again gathered on Friday evening at a barbeque cookout hosted by Georg and Erica Nockemann. It was a relaxed evening, and certainly helpful to me in an effort to take in all that had transpired over the near two weeks of my visit, and to prepare myself for the long voyage home to the United States.

Saturday

The trip would not have been complete without a walk down memory lane and a stop at *36 Disselhof Strasse*. On Saturday morning I visited with attorney Thomas Schwieren, the man who now owns the building that sits on my family's former property. In the afternoon we gathered at the home of my friend Anita Lane, and took advantage of the beautiful summer day and filmed an interview in her beautiful garden. Anita and her lovely daughters, Emily and Lovisa were charming hostesses.

Sunday

We were up early for what I thought would be a quiet breakfast. Much to my surprise all of my friends had once again gathered to say goodbye and wish me safe travels back to America. Those in attendance included the *Burgermeister* Bodo Klimpel and his wife as well as the official city entourage and most of the friends mentioned previously. Their presence made it quite difficult for me to leave. Needless to say, there were many tears shed that day by a good many of us.

Home

It is always good to return home from anywhere I travel. My humble apartment is filled with pictures of my parents, my family, and of good friends. These pictures are a source of great joy to me and are a constant reminder of what truly is important. I can only hope that God will grant me both the strength and the serenity to venture out of my apartment on a regular basis for many years to come, and that there will be many more trips to Germany and to other destinations so that I can share my tale of *The Gazebo* and to teach the children the message of tolerance.

AFTERWORD

Alex thought it was noteworthy for you, the reader, to know that Chapter 5 was actually the first chapter written at the beginning of the project. It was a natural place for me to start, especially after having heard the *Kristallnacht* story nearly a dozen times during the course of presentations at local schools and at the Virginia Holocaust Museum. Being proud of the chapter, I subsequently presented it as a sample of how I saw the book being put together. While the reading went well, and Alex was pleased with the result, as the project progressed, and my wife Susie and I tagged along with Alex to many of his presentations at various schools in the area, I still ended up re-writing this chapter more than a few times. With each passing revision, it became apparent to all of us just how emotionally charged the words contained in this narrative were to all of us engaged in this project. What had once been merely a story or historical account became as real and painful for us as it was for Alex almost seventy years ago. We attribute this to the fact that our love for Alex continued to grow during this same period. We felt his pain, his absolute terror, and the level of despair being experienced by the three Lebensteins as they hid first in the gazebo and then in the cemetery enclave, and attempted to place ourselves there along side of them, projecting what each of them must have been feeling most notably during that cold desolate period in the cemetery when death was mere inches away. No doubt, for Natan Lebenstein it was the taking of the final vestiges of any dignity he might have once mustered and retained.

For Lotte it was clearly pure terror and pain. For young Alex, it was the beginning of an incredibly cruel odyssey that few young people his age would survive, and it was also the end of his childhood, and the loss of innocence. When we later viewed still pictures of the enclave, and video of Alex actually sprawled on the ground in front of the enclave we felt the terror all the more.

Having sat with Alex on the porch of his apartment in the late fall and hearing the rustling of dried leaves on the sidewalk and watching his visible reaction to the sound that they make, leaves me no doubt that he still can recount the bone-chilling horror of that fateful night as easily as you and I might recall what we had for lunch yesterday. This is the lesson that must be taught to all that will listen to his message.

If it takes a village to raise a child, then it takes a whole lot of people to adequately capture the eighty one years of a remarkable life. Authoring, re-writing, editing, and editing some more, followed by more re-writing and editing, all go hand in hand and there have been many people who have contributed to this amazing work.

In the time that it has taken to compile and write this incredible story of triumph it has been my distinct pleasure *and honor* to spend countless hours with Alex Lebenstein. In that time we have become a part of one another's family, and along with Susie, Celeste, and a host of others, have shared many wonderful meals and times together. No matter how many times we go out to eat, or better yet, when Alex cooks for us, I am always surprised when in his favorite capacity of host he fixes a plate full of food as if for himself and then presents it to me in order "*that I should try it*" and broaden my horizons.

It bears noting that in the intervening years since the war, Alex has become very informed about a wide range of things. Most of our sessions in his apartment began with a check of the stock market – he had to know how his investments were doing. He is quite a brilliant conversationalist, and with his dry wit, his natural intelligence comes shining through. There is no doubt that given other circumstances he would have achieved a far different life. Nonetheless, he captivates those with whom he comes in contact, and that is largely due to his gregarious personality, a desire to please other people, as well as a natural inner brilliance. More often than not he will have an opinion on any topic ranging from politics to the economy. Largely self taught, it is hard to believe that this is not a formally educated man. In rebuttal he would say that it was purely a sense of self preservation and survival that has propelled him to do the things that he has done over the past sixty years. Because we have learned not to argue with Alex, we will leave it at that.

My life is forever changed for having known this great man, and while he may shake his finger at me, or slap the table as if seated at a *Stammtisch* in a local *Gasthaus* in disagreement after reading this, make no mistake, he is a <u>great</u> man. I have learned much about life, the desire to do good for others, and about simple gratitude from this man. He has helped me bring a greater perspective to my own existence and honed my skills to really prioritize what does and does not matter in this blink of an eye that we call Life. I suspect that he has done the same for the countless *thousands* of young people for whom he has take the time to address and to impart his wisdom, even if they are not aware of it at this point in their life.

Alex, nothing would make us happier than to be able to take you up on your offer of showing us Haltern am See the very next time that you return to Germany to visit with *your* [one thousand plus] *children*. Undoubtedly it will add yet another chapter to the never ending saga that we have come to embrace as much as if it were our own heritage, and our own legacy.

Perhaps the greatest thing about this entire experience has been the opportunity to watch an often tired, and sometimes ill, older gentleman summon   some hidden strength and seemingly change into a man twenty years his junior. Better yet, in playful moments, when with a twinkle in his eye and what we lovingly refer to as his "evil" laugh, he is once again transformed into that same little boy who was the only one mugging for the camera in kindergarten back in the darker days of 1933, or buying peanuts on the sly. Quick to greet one and all with arms opened wide and a kiss on the cheek, often including those he is meeting for the first time, all are made to feel at ease around this bear of a man.

Thank you to Alex and Celeste for a great 25th wedding anniversary dinner – and thanks for accepting our reservations for our 50th. We are counting on you to cook that one too! Hopefully we won't be grilling in the rain.

Thank you Alex for being a hero to many of us, and for insuring *that the children, politicians, and decision makers of future generations will know of this traumatic period in the history of mankind so that we can prevent it from ever occurring again.*

Don Levin

I never expected to be honored for anything in my life. To that end, I have spent most of my life feeling inferior to those around me. A mere three years of formal education will have that effect on a person. The time that I have spent in Germany since 1995 has generally been so overwhelming that it still resembles a dream. My trip there in 2008 would certainly fall into that category. I could never have imagined anything like being named an *Ehrenburger* or having a school named for me.

I have received many kind words as well as profuse thank you's from children, their parents, as well as educators in both the United States and Germany as they tell me how they have each benefitted from my efforts to teach tolerance and to make our little piece of the world a better place. I have received many other awards and accolades from other cities, civic organizations, and other associations, but nothing will come close to exciting me as much as when I see a glimmer of understanding in the eyes of a child. That is my ultimate reward.

As I continue to get older and my body sends me regular reminders of my age and my growing limitations, I am being forced to make choices on how to spend my remaining time. Since every day I wake is truly another gift from God, I am very comfortable using my remaining days as a teacher and speaker to the children of the new generation.

It remains my prayer that God will grant me many more years of life so that I can continue to teach the children this all important message.

Alex Lebenstein

Authors Acknowledgements

Telling a story such as Alex's is by far the most unique project that I have worked on to date. More than just a story, or tapestry of pictures and images, I had to often stop and remind myself that this was not merely an anonymous historical account but rather the record of his life!

As one might expect on a project of this scale, the memories of a man his age might not be as sharp and focused as desired. However, more often than not, as we peeled the onion and went through taping sessions, reading sessions, and editing sessions, details of memories long since forgotten, repressed, or safely hidden away, would come roaring back providing us greater insights. Sometimes a phone call to contemporaries on one continent or another would clarify or amplify points of contention.

Over the years since the end of the war there have been many of these historical accounts captured by other survivors and historians. Often time these records conflict with one another. We have attempted to be as accurate as possible, and to use only the most reliable of sources besides Alex's own memories. If however, there are any mistakes, misconceptions, or inaccuracies, they are unintentional.

As we captured Alex's life for all posterity, we did not want to over generalize the events, but attempted to provide the reader with an historical context so as to better understand the events as they happened and impacted the life of a young boy. We also tried to tell it from one man's view point rather than that of a country or certain group of people.

We both want to thank Susie Levin for her passion and compassion in bringing the two of us together in the beginning and for all of the encouragement, as well as for all of the questions that she asked during our taping sessions. An even larger thank you for having a vision of the project and keeping us on task even when we might lose our way or get bogged down in minutia or misunderstanding.

Thanks to Susie again, as well as Inge Horowitz and Jackie Tully, all of whom had a hand in the initial editing. A special thanks to John Hagadorn for his willingness to proofread and edit the manuscript when we had finally finished what we hoped would be a final draft. He was ably assisted by Wendy Spanier who brought a fresh set of eyes to the pages.

To my own children Phil, Karen, Katie, Jeff, and Eliese, who were enthusiastic about the project, especially after meeting Alex, or having their own classroom of students correspond with him. I hope the lessons revealed in this book touch their lives as they have my own.

Thanks also to other family, friends, and associates who encouraged the project or had a hand in reading, editing, and critiquing this work as it grew from concept to reality, session by session, page by page, draft by draft, all of us mindful of the importance attached to insuring that the children of future generations will know of this perspective of history.

Don Levin

Love and Thanks from Alex to:

I express my thanks to my sons, David and Daniel, who inspire me. My desires for their future have helped me make the change from hatred to love, and from bitterness to tolerance. My prayer is that they will perpetuate the message of love and tolerance through their families, students, and all whose lives they touch. Additionally I want to express my thanks and admiration to my grandson Adam and my granddaughter Lisa.

To my sister, Rose, and her husband Edward Spainer (both deceased), who sponsored me and convinced me, when I was yet very hesitant, to come to this great country. Rose and my sister, Alice, were able to escape the horror of incarceration and immigrated to England in 1939. As my only surviving family members, they gave me great love and support throughout the years. It is because of them that I have photo records and memorabilia, copies of which were destroyed on *Kristallnacht*. I also am grateful to my sister Alice's daughter, Jean Brodkey, who has honored me by inscribing the names of my parents on the tablets at Miami Beach Holocaust Memorial.

A special thanks to my angel, Miriam Davidow, to whom I owe my sanity. It was through her love, devotion and encouragement, that I was able to see past my own wounds and tragedies, and began to use them for good purposes rather than remain their victim. Her counsel enabled me to overcome the bitterness that was slowly eating away at me and to reach out to others by teaching tolerance and the dangers of indifference.

To Ernest Haas, who convinced me to reconsider my resolve never to have anything to do with the country of Germany. He discovered through a newspaper article that my hometown of Haltern am See was attempting to contact me in 1988. Because I refused to write or speak German, he took it upon himself to correspond with Haltern in my stead. It was because of this that the children of Haltern wrote to me, and began to soften my heart.

To all of my good friends in the City of Haltern am See, Germany. To Erwin and Tina Kirschenbaum for their warmth and generosity and friendship these many years, as well as Erwin's leadership on the various projects while he was Burgermeister. To Georg and Erica Nockemann who were so warm and hospitable and dedicated to making my many trips so wonderful. Erica, I don't know what I would have done without you as my translator especially during the first trips when my German was so poor. To teacher Hermann-Josef Teigelkamp of the Hans-Boeckler-Kollegschule. To former Burgermeister Josef Schmergal for his support of both my work and the activities of the students in the intervening years. To Gregor Husmann, the wonderful Archives Director for the City of Haltern, and the wonderful way in which he consistently maintains the archives and makes history come alive. To Anne Plum (nee Sondermann) and her son, Waldemar, and Monika, her daughter-in-law, for their continuing support and friendship. To Anita Lane and her daughters Emily and Lovisa who also have become so very dear to me. To Principal Michael Weiand, Associate Principals Franz-Joseph Berheide and Juergen Terschmitten, and the incredible faculty at the *Alexander-Lebenstein-Realschule* who have done so much to promote the education of tolerance. Special thanks to teachers and program sponsors Holger Freitag, Petra Seipelt, Maria Curti, Dr. Robert Seidel, Hans Peter Lau, Martin Herkt, and Thomas Sohn for their vision in bringing this important piece of history to their students. To Marcus Niehues, parent representative. To the outstanding student members of the various SV Teams over the years, but especially two young ladies, Anna Marie Uber and Femke Buensow, for their outstanding leadership, and Femke's added desire to learn more about the Holocaust by coming to Virginia and completing an internship at the VHM. Thanks also to School Superintendent Peter Burkowsky, and Sanem Kleff for serving so diligently as the head of the Action Courage program in Berlin. Thanks also to Dr. Josef Voz and Pastors Karl Hentschel and Bruno Pottebaum for their support. And finally, a very special and heartfelt thank you to Burgermeister Bodo Klimpel, the city elders, and the fine government of the city for bestowing these lasting honors upon me.

Celeste Kocen, my dear friend, who has encouraged all of the efforts relating to this book and whose suggestions have enriched it. Celeste has also been a support as I have traveled to various locations to make presentations.

To Inge Horowitz, who for years has helped me with correspondence and has been a strong support to me as I began to reach out to others and communicate tolerance to students, teachers, schools, and other community organizations. She did this in addition to the great work that she has done as President of the Emek Sholom Memorial Cemetery Organization. I admire her for her strength, dedication, and willingness to serve others.

To my family members, Esther Binshtok, David and Ellen Lebenstein and their son Adam, Celeste Kocen, and Lisa and Matthew Lipman, who have provided love, support and assistance to me on my various trips back to Germany and Latvia.

To Inge Horowitz, my son, David Lebenstein, Susie Levin, Jackie Tully, Wendy Spanier, John Hagadorn, and Marvin and Hanna Rosman, who have been an integral part of the editing process.

Finally, to Don Levin, the true author of the book, and his wife, Susie, for spending countless hours with me as I recalled the extreme horrors which I endured. Their friendship and love made it easier to recall memories that had been hidden away for many years. What began as work has evolved into a strong friendship filled with love and laughter. Susie also accompanies me to many of my speaking engagements so that I do not have to drive or set up my visual aids, helps me organize and preserve my materials, and to maintain my schedule. I do appreciate all that she does for me.

And for the many students, teachers and community leaders both in the United States and Germany who have encouraged me to put down on paper the story I told them in words during my presentations.

Alex Lebenstein

ABOUT THE AUTHORS

Alexander Lebenstein, is the sole surviving member of the Jewish community of the town of Haltern-am-See, Germany. Alex was born to Natan and Charlotte Lebenstein in the City of Haltern am See, Germany on 3 November 1927. He was their only son and the youngest of their four children.

At the time of *Kristallnacht,* or *Night of Broken Glass,* on November 9-10, 1938, when Adolf Hitler and the Nazi party openly began the persecution of the Jews of Germany, Alex was only a week past his eleventh birthday. During these terror-filled two days he and his parents were beaten by a roving gang of Nazis, stripped of all of their belongings, driven from their home, and forced to hide in a variety of places to include their garden gazebo and a ravine in the local cemetery, before finally finding refuge in the basement of a bed and breakfast at great risk to the owner. In the following days, they were, along with all of the other Jews remaining within the city, consigned to the newly established *ghetto*, where they would remain for over three years.

In January, 1942, Alex and his parents and the other two remaining Jews in Haltern were placed on a transport destined for the port city of Riga, Latvia, and the large ghetto established there. They endured a six day *cattle car* ride from Gelsenkirchen, Germany to Riga, Latvia. For six days, during one of the coldest winters experienced by Europe, they were crowded into this railroad car designed for the purpose of transporting cattle. Unheated, barren of seats or any sanitary facilities,

Alex witnessed first the fear of his fellow passengers and subsequently the death of several of those trapped inside with him.

From the ghetto within Riga, Alex was assigned to various *kommando groups* to perform slave labor in and around the city as well as within other satellite slave labor camps. All told, Alex labored in four different slave labor camps, with work assignments ranging from shoveling peat out of a bog to performing painting and refurbishing services to German Navy U-boats. He was fortunate to avoid death on several occasions, most notably when assigned to the concentration camps Stutthof and Kaiserwald.

In February, 1945, his final camp, Burggraben, was liberated by advancing Soviet troops. Ill with his second bout of typhus, Alex was actually too weak to remember liberation. Upon treatment and regaining his health, Alex served fellow prisoners for several months, assisting them to regain their health.

In September, 1945, Alex returned to Haltern am See, and shortly thereafter left it for the Displaced Persons Camp in Deggendorf (Bavaria) Germany.

In 1947, Alex came to the United States, and began a long and rewarding career as a butcher and entrepreneur. Retiring in 1999, he now dedicates his time to the teaching of children in both the United States and Germany on the topic of tolerance.

Alex is the proud father of two sons, and has two grandchildren, and two great-grandchildren.

In 2008 Alex had the honor of *Ehrenburger*, or honored person, bestowed upon him by the city of Haltern am See immediately before having the city's middle school renamed the *Alexander Lebenstein Realschule.* He is the first living person to have a school named for him.

Alex resides in Richmond, VA, and may be reached in care of the Virginia Holocaust Museum at <u>info@va-holocaust.com</u>.

Don Levin, is a former Attorney at Law with over thirteen years of general practice experience, and nine years as a court appointed arbitrator. He is also a retired U.S. Army officer, with over twenty three years of commissioned service spent in a variety of command and staff positions, twelve years of which were at the General Staff level. He is also a past senior sales leader for two Fortune 200 companies. He is currently President and CEO of a leadership coaching and executive search and placement company.

Don earned his JD from The John Marshall Law School, his MPA from the University of Oklahoma, and a BA from the University of Illinois-Chicago. He is also a graduate of the U.S. Army Command & General Staff College and the Defense Strategy Course, U.S. Army War College.

In his spare time, Don enjoys other forms of writing and is the author of the previously released military legal thriller *The Code,* the legal story *Broken Code,* as well as the historical fiction novel *Knight's Code.* He is also the co-author of the leadership book entitled *The Leader Coach: Exposing Your Soul.* He is currently working on several additional projects.

Don is very active with his church and within the community, and resides with his wife Susie, in Richmond, VA. They have five children and eight grandchildren, and two dogs named Barnes and Noble.

Don may be reached in care of <u>www.thegazebobook.com</u>.

Apppendix A

Erwin Kirschenbaum, former Mayor of Haltern am See, Germany, speaking to the faculty and student body at the Maggie L. Walker Governor's School, Richmond, Va. on November 6, 2002.

Dr. Roberts, Faculty and students,
Thank you very much for the warm welcome.

I'm deeply honoured to be invited to this year's Prejudice Awareness Summit, especially as I have the opportunity to speak to you alongside such a distinguished person and veritable symbol for this summit, Dr. Terrence Roberts.
What I would like to talk about this morning is the project "School Without Racism, School With Courage" that is launched in several European countries and that the Realschule Haltern in my native town on the northern border of the Ruhr area in Germany also participates in.

The movement for a School Without Racism began in 1988 in Antwerp in Belgium when some young people wanted to do something against both: the growing racism and the rise of the extreme right wing in politics which tried to bring back old Nazi ideas that seemed to have been overcome in the democracies of Europe.

Some students, teachers and organizers decided that the best place to act was the school. Every young boy or girl at a certain time of life goes to school and the idea was to apply to young people whose personalities were still fragile.

Today antiracist education has been inserted into school's everyday activities in more than 500 schools in Europe. More than 140 schools take part in Germany.

How does this project work?

An SWR is a school:

- without either discrimination or racism

- where genuine information about immigrants is given in an objective way

- where the study of other cultures is made not only on a cognitive basis but also on an affective basis to abolish racism

- where racial organisations and propaganda are forbidden

- where common activities on both - racism and a multicultural society – are organized by pupils, parents , teachers and headships.

All this begins with the signing of the call for a SWR, a declaration which is drafted by the schools along the lines of their countries' SWR secretariat.

The school may become a SWR when at least 70 % of teachers, headships and pupils (with the parents' consent) have signed the call and activities along these lines have been carried out.

I'll give you an impression of what the Realschule did in order to get this title and the plaque which is then put in a prominent position on the outside of the school building to show everyone which spirit is ruling this school.

To put things into perspective for you I must explain that a Richmond citizen, Mr Alexander Lebenstein, who is present today and a dear friend of mine, contributed immensely to preparing the ground in my native town Haltern am See.

Mr Lebenstein is the only Haltern Jewish citizen who survived the Holocaust. He went to America after he was liberated and in 1995 he returned for a visit to his native Haltern when he was invited by students to tell them his story about the dreadful and inhuman atrocities that were committed by the Nazis in the German name.

His visit and the emotional and fruitful encounters between him and students of Haltern sparked off a renewed interest not only in Haltern's history during the so called III.Reich but also in what means we can develop to avoid such a disaster to humanity now and for future times.

The Realschule students took up this discussion and in the last two years staged the following events to name but a few:

- An exhibition of posters with the title "Posters against Violence and Racism"

- An exhibition with the title " We will not forget " about Kristallnacht, the progrom against Jews in 1938

- A talk with an eye-witness to the Nazi terror

- An event called " There was no return from this station" The school set up an info-board at the station in Haltern to remind passengers of the trains going to Auschwitz and other concentration camps.

- Invitation and talk with three former members of forced labour from the Netherlands

- Anti-violence training

- "Aysche and Richard," a theatre play against prejudice and discrimination

- Students collect money for a Turkish girl suffering from leukaemia

- Parents', teachers' and students' recital from literary works that the Nazis banned and burned.

- Visits from groups coming from South Africa and Tansania

- Sculptures and paintings "Bridges of Friendship"

- 9/11 condolence book sent to American embassy

- Holocaust Remembrance Day: classes enact episodes from Haltern's history between 1933 – 1945 in the town where they originally took place

What courage these students showed to do the walk to the station where the Jewish citizens were sent to the concentration camp from or to be driven through the town with a poster round your neck telling everyone you were a friend of Jews.

But the students finally achieved their goal. They got the title SWR which was presented in Haltern only this year.
The students were keen to vote Alexander Lebenstein to be their mentor on the way to keep up the obligation that is connected with this project:

The SWR project is never complete. The school population may change but the plaque out on the school walls makes it clear to everybody which way the school would like to follow.

Students, teachers and parents must do their best to find and establish new groups to carry on the work in their school.

I could dwell on more aspects of this project but as a former mayor of Haltern who was grateful and happy to be able to help a few things get off the ground I know that a speech should not be too long.
But let me make one suggestion to conclude this talk: It would be very helpful if we could link up the fine work you are doing here with the existing European network of SWR. This could be the start of a global outlook and hope for a better future.

Thank you very much for your attention.

APPENDIX B

List of Pictures

Group 1

1. Grandfather Alexander Lebenstein.
2. Grandmother Henrietta Lebenstein.
3. Grandfather Alexander Lebenstein's butcher shop at 36 Disselhof Strasse. Note the "A. Lebenstein" sign that is hanging over the door. The sign is now on display in the rail car on the grounds of the Alexander-Lebenstein-Realschule. A young Natan Lebenstein is now operating the shop since the death of his father.
4. young Lotte Josephs before her marriage to Natan Lebenstein.
5. Natan and Lotte Lebenstein, undated.
6. Alex as a baby with his mother and three sisters.
7. Alex as a baby.
8. Alex as a toddler.
9. Kindergarten 1933. Note the Nazi flags in the rear of the picture and the glum countenance on the faces of all the children with

the exception of the curly haired Alex who is clearly mugging for the camera.

10. First day of school.
11. Alex and his parents and two sisters in front of the family garden gazebo.
12. Alex, age 9.
13. Alex "smoking" in his lederhosen.
14. Alex in apron, ready to assist in the butcher shop.
15. Farm Butcher
16. Alex the shepherd in the backyard at Disselhof 36. The fence in the background is the same fence against which they caught their breath and nursed their wounds on the night of *Kristallnacht*
17. Alex with his parents at the time of his Bar Mitzvah while residing in the *Judenhaus.*
18. Six year old Alex in front of the gazebo with sister Rose (left) and Alice (right) and two neighbors.
19. Disselhof 36, home and butcher shop in happier days.
20. Alex in the family vegetable garden with his sisters
21. . The resulting destruction of the Haltern Synagogue in the aftermath of *Kristallnacht,* November 10, 1938.
22. Signing over the remaining Jewish property in the City of Haltern on April 29, 1941. This document bears the signature of "Natan Israel Lebenstein." The middle name of "Israel" had been added to the birth certificates of all Jewish men. "Sarah" was added to that of all Jewish women. The signature of the witness has been inked out. This document is still a part of the City Archives.
23. The last five remaining Jews residing in Haltern were designated for transport in January, 1942. Unable to pay the individual 50DM fee charged for this service, Natan Lebenstein was directed to the City Hall where his declaration on behalf of himself, his wife Lotte, son Alex, Frau Jenny Kleeberg, and Hermann Cohen was duly noted and recorded for the archives. The signature of the official has also been inked over in this document.
24. An identity again. On 20 September 1945, Alex regained his name and identity. The only difference between this identification

card and one issued during the Nazi reign is the absence of the Eagle and Swastika.

25. Alex in the Fall of 1945.
26. Group photo taken in Displaced Persons (DP) Camp Deggendorf.
27. Crazy man in the kitchen, Alex proudly wearing his apron in Camp Deggendorf where he found a niche in the camp kitchen.
28. February, 1947. Alex in the grocery store on Nine Mile Road in Richmond, VA. With him are his sister Rose and brother-in-law Edward Spanier, and niece Esther.

Group 2

29. Welcome sign greeting Alex at the Haltern Realschule.
30. Placard sign for Schule Ohne Rassismus, Schule Mit Courage (School without Racism, School with Courage.) This is a national recognition bestowed on select schools throughout Germany that meet strict criterion. See Appendix A.
31. Cover of the book compiled by students at the Realschule that was later sold on the streets of Haltern at a cost of 10 DM. *1995 Haltern: Die Gesichte Der Juden im Haltern (The History of the Jews in Haltern).*
32. Newspaper ad promoting the Realschule's activities and Alex's support of the projects with his presence in Haltern.
33. Alex speaking at Ort gegen das Vergessen (The Place of No Return) commemorating the departing Jews from the City of Haltern.
34. Ort gegen das Vergessen – Place of No Return.
35. Exterior of the 1908 vintage cattle car acquired and refurbished by the students at the Realschule as a lasting memorial to all those who perished during the persecution of the Jews.

36. When the railroad car was relocated from a station siding to the grounds of the Realschule the work was done by the Mertmann Company completely free of charge. Principal Michael Weiand (center) honors the company for their generosity.
37. Inside the cattle car: a display that depicts Jewish life before, during, and after Hitler. Note the side by side pictures of Natan and Lotte Lebenstein previously depicted in this book.
38. The cemetery marker purchased by the students of the Realschule with proceeds of the book *Die Gesichte Der Juden im Haltern*. The acknowledgment that Alex survived is unfortunately lost in the grass.
39. Students marching in commemoration of *Kristallnacht*. Burgermeister Erwin Kirschenbaum is in the foreground with his camera.
40. Students marching in commemoration of *Kristallnacht*
41. Up close and personal with Alex.
42. Alex being swarmed by his adoring children
43. Teaching from his large book of articles, pictures, and other memorabilia at Virginia Commonwealth University in Richmond, VA.
44. Alex with sons David and Danny at Shea Stadium in New York.
45. A triumphant Alex leaving the opening of the cattle car memorial on the grounds of the Realschule. He is reacting to the following picture.
46. The children of the Realschule express their feelings for godfather Alex.
47. The superstar-laden soccer team of Schalke 04 protests against racism.
48. The Star of David figures prominently in another commemoration of Kristallnacht conducted by the students of the Realschule.
49. Alex and 91-year old Frau Plum (nee Sondermann) owner and operator of the Hotel in which Alex and his family sought refuge on the night of November 10, 1938.
50. Alex with Erwin and Tina Kirschenbaum in Richmond, VA on one of their visits to the United States.

51. Stolpersteine that introduces the project as a remembrance to those who lived through or perished in the horrors of 1933-1945.
52. The *Stolpersteine* (stumbling stones) being added to the sidewalks and streets of Haltern by Gunter Demnig.
53. The three stones commemorating Natan, Lotte, and Alex Lebenstein in front of Disselhof 36.
54. Alex examining the stones in front of Disselhof 36 on one of his visits.
55. Thomas Schwieren, the owner of the newly constructed Disselhof 36 and the commemorate plaque that honors the Lebenstein family.
56. The plaque that can be seen by pedestrians as they pass the new Disselhof 36.
57. Planting Alex's apple tree on the grounds of the Realschule.
58. Alex's apple tree will someday provide shade for the memorial to those who perished during the Holocaust.
59. Tears of Isieu being formed in front of the cattle car by collecting drops of melting ice.
60. Stones with the names representing each of the 44 French children from the town of Isieu who were murdered by the Nazis in 1944.
61. The Virginia Holocaust Museum receives its own cattle car.
62. Elie Wiesel and Eliese Levin, one of Alex's new children, during one of Dr. Wiesel's visits to Richmond, VA.
63. Alex and Elie Wiesel
64. Alex celebrates his 80th birthday on November 3, 2007.
65. Memorial at Riga –Bikernieki with ancillary stones that have names of known and presumed victims of the mass killings that took place in 1941-1942.
66. Alex with Georg and Erica Nockemann in Haltern.
67. Alex and war-time friend Ewald Aul holding pictures of themselves taken at the end of the war in 1945.
68. Burgermeister Bodo Klimpel at the time of the Ehrenburger ceremonies.
69. The Ehrenburger certificate.

70. Alex holds the Ehrenburger (honored citizen) declaration filled with the signatures of all the city elders.
71. Alex and Realschule Principal Michael Weiand.
72. The Alexander-Lebenstein-Realschule of Haltern am See is unveiled.
73. Alex Lebenstein and Don Levin, celebrating the completion of the editing process.

We gratefully acknowledge all those who contributed pictures for this work.

APPENDIX C

Index of References and Footnotes

As noted, the stories contained in the book are based on the memories of Alex Lebenstein. The following sources were used to verify his accounts and to assist in establishing the historical context in which the stories take place. Any discrepancies are unintentional.

Borowski, Tadeusz, *This Way for the Gas, Ladies and Gentlemen,* New York, Penguin Books, 1976

Gilbert, Martin, *Atlas of the Holocaust,* NewYork, William Morrow & Co., 1993

The Holocaust Chronicle, Lincolnwood, IL, Publications International Ltd, 2003

Ward, Geoffrey C and Burns, Ken, *the War: An Intimate History 1941- 1945,* Alfred A. Knopf, New York, 2007

Winter, Alfred, *The Ghetto of Riga and Continuance,* 1998, privately published

World Book Encyclopedia

The United States Holocaust Memorial Museum
100 Raoul Wallenberg Place, SW
Washington, DC 20024-2126
Main telephone: (202) 488-0400
TTY: (202) 488-0406
http://www.ushmm.org

The Virginia Holocaust Museum
2000 East Cary Street
Richmond, VA 23223-7032
(804) 257-5400
info@va-holocaust.com

Footnotes

1. Germany Population, 31 March 2007. German Population trends. http://www.country-data.com/cgi-bin/query/r-4901.html

2. German Jewish Refugees, 1933-1939, 31 March 2007. Holocaust Encyclopedia. <http://www.ushmm.org/wlc/article.php?lang=en&ModuleId=10005468.>

3. Virginia Holocaust Museum

4. The Holocaust Chronicle, p.144